Introduction to 737

Conforti, Facundo Jorge
   Introduction to 737 / Facundo Jorge Conforti. - 1a ed. - Mar del Plata :
Facundo Jorge Conforti, 2021.
   200 p. ; 21 x 14 cm.

   1. Aviación. 2. Aviones. 3. Aeronáutica. I. Título.
   CDD 629.13334042

Fecha de Catalogación: 01/02/2021

Introduction to 737

.

Facundo Conforti, 2022.

Preface

Welcome to a new edition of the most successful collection of aeronautical books in America. At the request of readers around the world, we have created this magnificent literary work about everything that a pilot in training must learn about one of the most flown aircraft in the world, the magnificent Boeing 737. With the collaboration of Captain Aldo Tatoli, with more than 30 years of airline experience, we have developed an educational manual based on the models B737-700, B737-800 and B737-900.

An educational guide that will take the reader to know the main components of the aircraft, its systems and the operation principle of each. A work based on the extensive experience of Captain Aldo Tatoli, who has commanded B737 in almost all its versions.

An unparalleled contribution to the aeronautical market, where pilots and fans demand more and more information and material to study dayly. A work that promises to be the starting point for many more titles about this great aircraft.

Our special thanks to Captain Aldo Tatoli for his participation, his dedication to teaching and his enormous passion for aviation.

Facundo Conforti   *Aldo Tatoli*
Editor Biblioteca Aeronáutica   Capitán B737

Contents

The New era

With the arrival of jet engines, a new era had arrived for world aviation. This new way of building airplanes would not replace the traditional engines powered by huge propellers but would begin a new stage in aircraft manufacturing in different models.

By the end of the 1960s, the aeronautical industry had advanced in such a way that no one considered that it could go beyond. The great pioneers continued to manufacture innovative aircraft powered by jet engines as the newest on the market and engines powered by traditional propellers. On these two variants of power plants, large manufacturers varied their models in passenger capacity, autonomy, short, medium and long-range performance.

The trade war had become an excessive struggle between the airlines. In the main market, the United States, PANAM airline added aircraft to its fleet steadily and demanded that its main supplier, Boeing, design and build new models that make a difference. It was then at the end of 1960 that the factory launched its two masterpieces, the B737 and the B747! Let's know the history of one of these Boeing emblems.

Boeing 737 is born

In the era of the aeronautical revolution of new aircraft with better power plants, better performance and greater capacity than the aircraft of the previous decade, the industry demanded constant progress from its operators. Thus, the first commercial battle to obtain this new Boeing model was not won by an American company, but by the German airline Lufthansa anticipating PANAM in the purchase of the first model of the new Boeing 737. On February 19, 1965, Boeing announced its intention to build the MODEL 737, a short-range transport powered by two turbofans. The first Boeing 737-100 made its first flight on April 9, 1967 and Lufthansa inaugurated its services with this plane on February 10, 1968.

The new B737 model consisted of the fuselage of the Boeing 727 with a tail configuration similar to the Boeing 707. A capacity of 60 to 85 passengers was expected, but Lufthansa, who placed the first order, needed a capacity of 100 seats. Because of this, the fuselage was conveniently extended. The wing incorporated much of the technology developed for the 727, and the area of greatest changes was given by the power plant. It was decided to mount the engines on the wing because there was no space in the short fuselage and because passengers cannot sit near the engines mounted on the fuselage.

Two months after Boeing launched the 737, the company announced the simultaneous development of the larger capacity 737-200 model. The first 737-200 flew on August 8, 1967 and the entry into service occurred with United Airlines on April 29, 1968. The

737-200 had a fuselage 1.83 m (6 feet) longer than the previous model to accommodate 130 passengers.

The rapid growth of air traffic, and therefore the capabilities of the planes that existed at that time, meant that there was practically no demand for the 737-100 (100-103 seats) so production ended after only 30 units had been built.

The relatively short takeoffs and landings of the 737 made it suitable to operate from small regional airports, and even from unpaved airfields. That is why Boeing developed an appropriate FOD (Foreign Object Damage) protection for airplanes. The years passed and it seemed that the new model of the Boeing firm was going to exceed all the records expected and achieved by previous and competing models. Although the first commercial conquest of the B737 was in the hands of Lufthansa, the first symbolic achievement was from the company

United Airlines which managed to buy the model of B737 number 100 built by the factory.

After its innovative B737-200 model, Boeing launches a more advanced version known as B737-200 Advanced. This new version launched in 1979 had greater autonomy and takeoff weight, and was built with composite materials and equipped with the most advanced avionics system of the time.

Already in the 1980s, Boeing decided to bring more life to its B737 line and launched the new 737 series known as Boeing 737 Classic. This series is composed of three emblems of the firm, the B737-300, the B737-400 and the B737-500.

They were distinguished by new technologies such as New CFM-56 turbofan engines, which were 20% more efficient than the JT8D used in the original version. The redesigned wings, improvements in aerodynamics, and improvements in the cockpit, with the option of the addition of the EFIS (Electronic Flight Instrumentation System) system. The passenger cabin similar to the one used in the Boeing 757. The maximum speed for which this type of aircraft reaches the transonic regime is the critical Mach number, whose approximate value was 0.8M.

For its part, the legendary B737-200, already with too much history on its back and with a technology that was becoming obsolete in the face of so much progress in the industry, production of 200 ended in 1988 after 1,114 units were manufactured. The 1980s had been a great success for the B737 saga in its Classic version. With worldwide sales records, the factory continued to build models and with a constantly growing aeronautical market. In 1993 Boeing gave rise to talk again. In the same year it launched the new series of the B737 named B737

Next Generation. A new saga of models that included the B737-600, B737-700, B737-800 and B737-900.

It is characterized by having new technologies such as Updating CFM-56-7 engines, being 7% more effective than the 3 series used in the classic line. The wings were completely redesigned, increasing their width and area, among other improvements. Increase in fuel storage capacity, and also increase in the maximum take-off weight. The newly redesigned cockpit, with 6 LCD screens along with the latest avionics technology. Cabin improvements, improved range and optimized for international travel.

The years followed their natural course and the success of the B737 Next Generation saga had no limits. Already in a market with greater competition from other large manufacturers such as Airbus and the A320 Family line, the production of the B737 demanded greater agility in deliveries, lower manufacturing cost and greater results in in-flight performances.

The confrontation between elite manufacturers had become a fight of two, there was no other manufacturer that could compete with the B737 saga and the A320 line. Between them was the battle. Both firms improved their models year after year, seeking to gain some competitive advantage over their competitor. The aeronautical industry was no longer so young, the year 2000 had arrived and soon after came the first 100 years of aviation life. A cycle of experiences, mistakes and learning that led manufacturers to perfect their techniques and equipment more and more.

Since 2006, Boeing had been studying different proposals to replace its Boeing 737 model, in a project called Boeing Y1, which would accompany the Boeing 787 Dreamliner. The decision on the launch of this program was postponed, and delayed until 2011. However, in 2010, Airbus launched the Airbus A320 Neo, a variant derived from the original A320, which incorporated a new, more efficient power plant with lower operating costs. This decision was well received by numerous airlines, which placed numerous orders for this new aircraft. This caused Boeing's board of directors to approve on August 30, 2011, a renewing project with which to compete with Airbus, called Boeing 737 MAX.

Boeing claimed that the 737 MAX offered a consumption of 16% lower than the current Airbus A320 aircraft and 4% lower than the Airbus A320 Neo. The three models of the new variant were the 737 MAX 7, the 737 MAX 8 and the 737 MAX 9, which were based on the 737-700, 800 and 900ER respectively, which in turn were the best-selling models in the 737 Next Generation range.

Systems I

B737-700/800/900

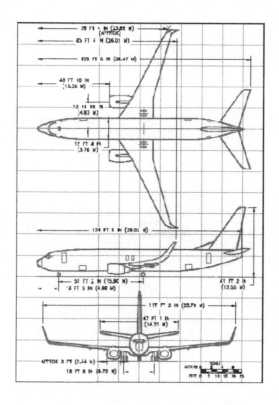

Introduction

The theoretical study of an aircraft is undoubtedly the starting point of every pilot for learn how to fly an airplane. The successful Boeing 737 model series has evolved over the years, but always maintaining the simplicity of its flight systems and operations, characteristics that place the B737 as one of the most sought-after aircraft in the world by airlines. This manual bases all its content on the systems and operations of the models: B737-700/800/900, making the differences when necessary and highlighting the virtues of each of these excellent aircraft.

Dimensions, limitations and weights

The first considerations when studying an aircraft are to know the values of its dimensions, basic limitations and weights. This information is analysed below for each model of B737-700/800/900.

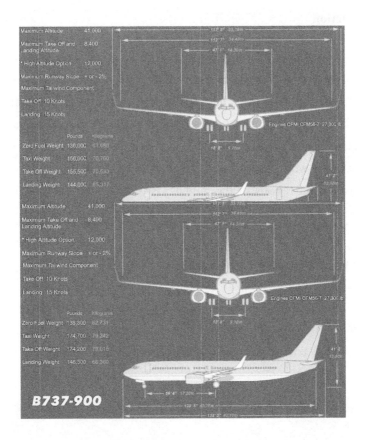

Analysing the three models of 737, the dimensions have increased in each of them. Perhaps one of the most important is the length of the aircraft, wherein the 700 model it starts at 33.60 meters, in the 800 model it extends to 39.50 meters and in the 900 model it extends again to 42.10 meters. This increase in its dimensions allows you a larger number of passengers and cargo in warehouses, depending on the configuration chosen by each company.

Regarding the main operational limitations, there are no changes between the three models, maintaining the same line of performance. As for weights, they are values that have evolved in each model. Using as an example takeoff and landing weights (TOW) (LW), the 700 model offers a TOW of 57,606 kilograms and an LW of 54,657 kilograms. For its part, the 800 model increases these values by TOW 70,533 kilograms and LW 65,317 kilograms. Finally, the 900 model outstrips itself by offering a TOW of 79,015 kilograms and an LW of 66,360 kilograms. It should be considered that they are referential values and could vary depending on the equipment requested by each airline.

One of the main operational considerations between each model is the turning radius of the nose and tail of the plane. The larger the fuselage, the more the radius of rotation of the aircraft will increase. Faced with this situation, the pilot must keep these values in mind, since there may be the opportunity to fly several models at the same time, that is, on the same working day, and in the face of the change in the turning radius, it is extremely necessary to know the values of each aircraft.

The nose and tail turning radius of each aircraft model is detailed below: 737-700, 737-800 and 737-900. Note the increase in each turning radius as the aircraft model has advanced.

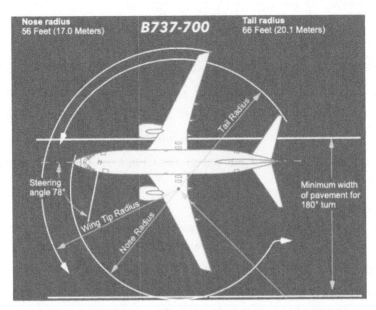

Nose radius
56 Feet (17.0 Meters)

B737-700

Tail radius
66 Feet (20.1 Meters)

Tail Radius

Steering
angle 78°

Wing Tip Radius

Nose Radius

Minimum width
of pavement for
180° turn

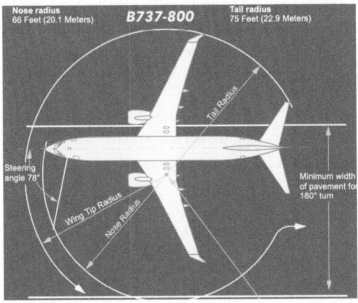

Nose radius
66 Feet (20.1 Meters)

B737-800

Tail radius
75 Feet (22.9 Meters)

Tail Radius

Steering
angle 78°

Wing Tip Radius

Nose Radius

Minimum width
of pavement for
180° turn

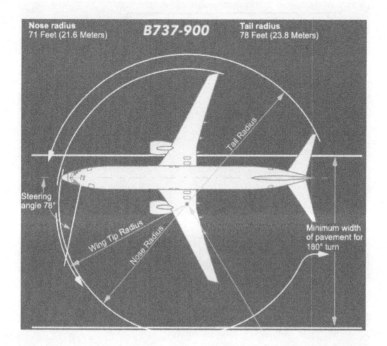

Flight deck

The cockpit of the three models does not present great variations. It is composed of two upper panels known as "Overhead Panel", a flight panel named "Glareshield" where in this case, it can present two variables depending on the equipment that each company wants. In the central section the main panel that combines analog and digital instruments that work in conjunction with a lower panel known as the "Pedestal Panel" where the acceleration quadrant of the aircraft is located. Control knobs maintain Boeing's traditional style with control columns and pedals under the main panel.

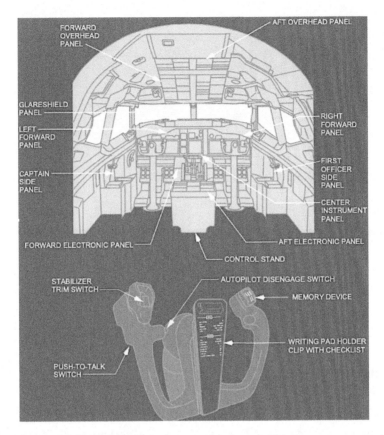

A cockpit design that has evolved over the years compared to its predecessors, but that has been outstrippedby the total renovation of the cabin offered by the 737 MAX version taking a chance on a complete "Glass Cockpit".

From the front of the cockpit, observing towards the exit of it, various devices are part of the cockpit.

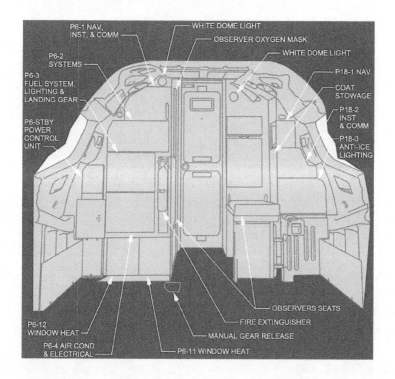

Overhead panel

The upper panel is divided into two sections, the front upper panel or "Forward Overhead Panel" and the rear upper panel or "Afterward Overhead Panel". In these panels most of the aircraft's systems are concentrated and are operated by the pilots, depending on the roles they perform at each moment of the flight.

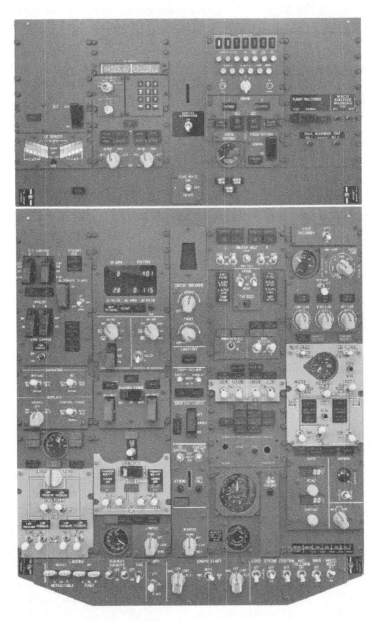

Each section of the panel and its respective operation will be analysed in later chapters.

Glareshield

It consists of a central panel divided into three sections. The main section where pilots can select the flight mode to be made, hence its name "Mode Control Panel" or MCP. On the sides are two EFIS system control panels, one for each pilot and known as "EFIS Control Panel" or ECP. And finally, on the sides are two warning panels, one for each pilot.

Most flight functions operated by the pilots are located in the MCP and can have two variants for the 737 model, depending on the manufacturer of this equipment.

From the MCP, pilots can control the course, speed, altitude, autopilot, flight modes, vertical speed, and various other functions.

Flight mode control panel

As mentioned above, the MCP, or mode control panel, offers two variants depending on the manufacturer of the equipment, but both models offer the same functions and location of buttons and switches, exactly. The MCF of the Collins model is detailed below.

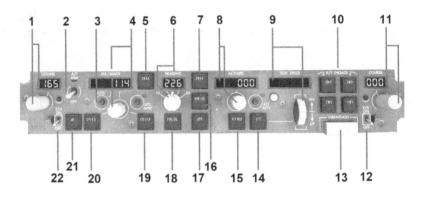

1. Left side (captain) course selection rotating knob.
2. Auto Throttle system activation switch.
3. Speed unit change switch between KT and MACH.
4. Manually selected speed information window
5. Vertical navigation mode activation button.
6. Swivel target selection knob. It has two scales of operation, 1 in 1 and 10 in 10. Above the knob is the computer window of the manually selected course.
7. Lateral navigation mode activation button.
8. Rotating altitude selection knob and information window.
9. Vertical speed value selection swivel wheel and information window.
10. Autopilot activation buttons A and B in different modes.
11. Right side turntable course selection knob (First Officer).

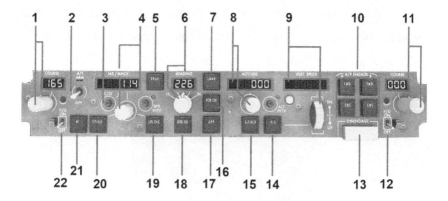

15. Altitude Hold mode activation button. When activated, the aircraft will stop the ascent or descent to level in that instance.

16. VOR or LOC mode activation button in automatic flight.

17. APP Approach mode activation button.

18. HDG heading mode activation button in automatic flight.

19. Level Change mode activation button. When activated, the aircraft will be able to change flight level while maintaining the current speed.

20. SPEED SPD mode activation button, granting speed control to autopilot.

21. N1 activation button. When activated, the auto throttle system will take the power to the pre-defined limit of the N1 value.

22. FD (flight director) activation knob on the captain's side.

The ECP offers various functions, such as the selection of EFIS views, stopovers, radio aids, and other modes of flight. There is a CCA for each pilot located on the sides of the MCP.

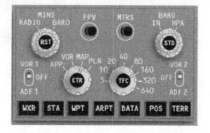

Lastly, the glareshield ends at the tips with warning panels that include Fire Warning, Master Caution, and system alarms. Like the ECP, there is a panel for each pilot at the ends of the glareshield.

Main Panel

The main panel is divided into three sections, a central one (Central Forward Panel or CFP) and two lateral ones, one for the captain (Left Forward Panel or LFP) and one for the first officer (Right Forward Panel or RFP). In these panels are located the main flight, navigation and systems screens..

The center section consists of additional flight instruments that function as alternative or "backup" instruments. This instrument section can be made up of several analog instruments or a single digital one. In the centre is a display that provides all the information about the parameters of the engines and is known as the Upper DU (display unit). On the DU is the automatic braking system and on the right is the landing gear drive lever.

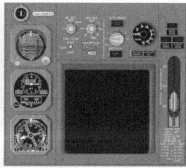

On the sides of the centre section are the side panels composed of two main screens, a primary flight display or PFD (primary flight display) and a navigation screen or ND (navigation display). These screens offer the same information for both pilots at the same time, although the navigation screen has the possibility of configuring different kinds of views independently on each side.

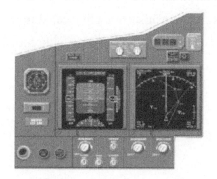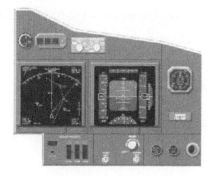

Both panels have a stopwatch and a screen brightness adjustment section. Only in the right panel is a braking pressure indicator incorporated.

Pedestal Panel

The bottom panel is divided into three sections. The front section is composed of a display that offers information on engine systems and parameters, and, on its sides, are two flight computers where pilots load all the information about flight plan, performance, weather and data relevant to the operation. The centre section is composed of the acceleration quadrant, which contains the operation of engine power, the flap system, the reverser system, the speed brake system and the "Trimm" system with a manual and/or automatic operation wheel.

This central section includes the panel of the fire protection system where the fire extinguisher activation mechanisms are located for both engines and the APU. Finally, in the rear section are located the radio communication and radio navigation systems, along with the transponder, the meteorological radar operation panel and the operation of the cabin lights.

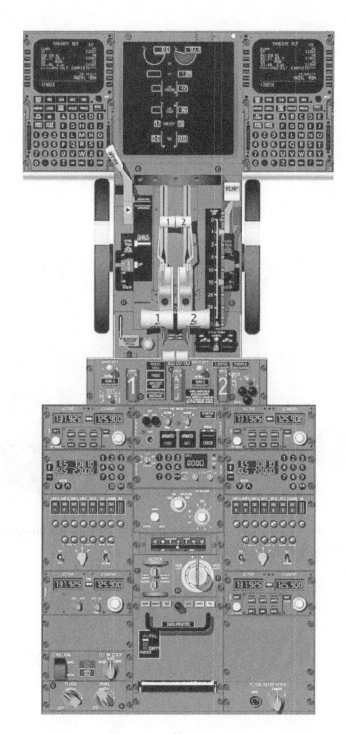

31

Light Systems

The aircraft's outdoor light system offers a wide variety of lighting that facilitates night or low visibility operations. This system is operated manually from the top panel or overhead panel, where on the sides of the bottom are located a set of knobs that operate each lighting function.

In the left margin is the light panel that includes: landing lights, runway turnoff lights and taxi lights..

Retractable Landing Lights: A powerful light system with a pair of headlights that extend from the fuselage downwards and retract when the pilot wants to turn off the light system.

Fixed Landing Lights: A system of shorter-range lights with a pair of extendable headlights, just like the previous lights.

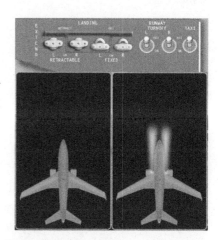

Runway Turnoff Lights: A system of powerful lights facing diagonally to the longitudinal axis of the aircraft to facilitate and illuminate the taxiways during the rotation of the aircraft.

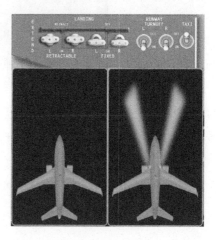

Taxi Lights: A single headlamp that emits a light in a straightforward line to illuminate the taxiway on which the aircraft is moving.

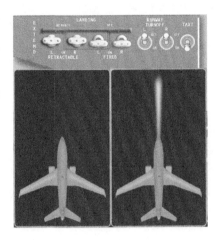

On the right margin is another light panel that includes: logo lights, strobe lights, anti-collision lights, wings lights and wheel lights.

Logo Lights: A system of lights that direct the lighting towards the tail of the plane to illuminate the company logo.

Position Lights: A system of navigation lights that offers two modes. A static light mode and a combined light mode that incorporates a system of strobe lights. The static lights have a red light on the edge of the left wing and a green light on the edge of the right wing.

Anti Collision Lights: A single red flashing light headlamp is located above the fuselage. This light is turned on when the aircraft is about to start retracement and start the engines.

Wing Lights: A system of lights that direct the lighting towards the wings to give the pilot the possibility of visual verification of the wing surface.

Wheel Lights: A system of lights that illuminates the landing gear assembly to facilitate its verification by ground personnel.

Regarding the lighting of the interior of the cockpit, from the main panel, pilots can adjust the lighting intensity of flight displays by operating the screen brightness commands from the bottom of each panel. This lighting system is independent of each panel, for both the captain and the first officer.

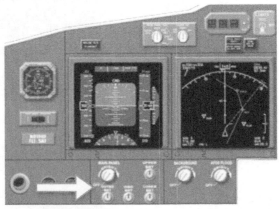

Finally, from the bottom panel, you can control the lighting intensity of all the main panels and the intensity of an upper reflector that illuminates the cabin in general.

In addition to the traditional system of lights, interior and exterior, there is an emergency light system that offers three optional modes: off mode, armed mode and on mode. In armed mode, the emergency light system is automatically activated when the aircraft's electrical system fails. Just below the emergency light panel are the two knobs that activate the "do not smoke" and "adjust seat belts" light signal.

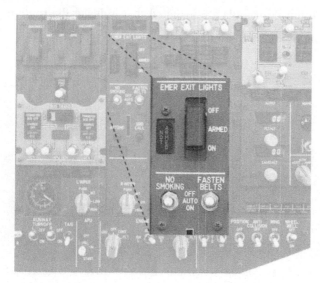

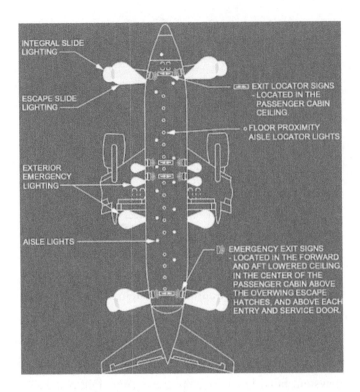

INTEGRAL SLIDE LIGHTING

ESCAPE SLIDE LIGHTING

EXTERIOR EMERGENCY LIGHTING

AISLE LIGHTS

EXIT LOCATOR SIGNS - LOCATED IN THE PASSENGER CABIN CEILING.

FLOOR PROXIMITY AISLE LOCATOR LIGHTS

EMERGENCY EXIT SIGNS - LOCATED IN THE FORWARD AND AFT LOWERED CEILING, IN THE CENTER OF THE PASSENGER CABIN ABOVE THE OVERWING ESCAPE HATCHES, AND ABOVE EACH ENTRY AND SERVICE DOOR.

The objective of the emergency lights inside the aircraft is to illuminate the escape routes before an evacuation. Along the central corridor, bright light rails are installed that indicate the route to follow in the event of an evacuation.

EFIS System

The EFIS (Electronic Flight Instrument System) system is composed of a series of digital screens or displays that offer all the information that traditional instruments but in a comprehensive way. On the one hand, there are flight control and navigation displays, and on the other hand there are system control displays and engine parameters. Each of these displays is known as DU (display unit) and is classified as follows:

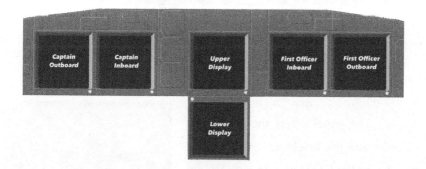

All the information presented in each DU comes from two sources known as DEU 1 (display electronic unit) and DEU 2, which obtain information from all the aircraft's sensors and systems. The DEU 1 supplies the captain's side and the upper display, while the DEU 2 supplies the captain's side and the lower display. In case of failure of any of the DEU, the other will be able to supply the entire system.

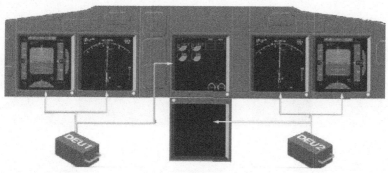

The EFIS system has several control panels in the main panel, above the glareshield and the overhead panel. The brightness of the screens is controlled independently by each pilot from the rotating knobs in the control panel located under the flight displays.

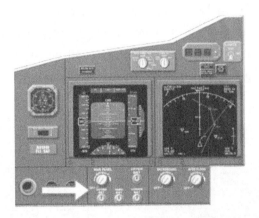

The panel offers the possibility of adjusting the brightness of the main panel, and the brightness of each DU on the operating side and the central DUs.

Above the overhead panel are the EFIS system font and screen control panel. From the left section, a rotating knob allows you to select the sources that will control the entire EFIS system, whether source 1 or DEU 1, source 2 or DEU 2, or in the automatic position where each DEU controls its corresponding side.

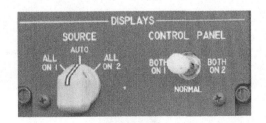

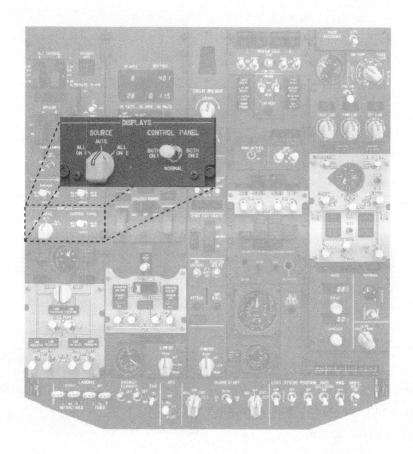

In the right section of the panel, there is a switch that allows you to select the EFIS control panel that will command the system. In the NORMAL position, the captain controls his screens with his control panel and the first officer controls his screens with his own control panel. In the BOTH ON 1 position, the screens of both pilots are controlled by the same panel, on the captain's side. In the BOTH ON 2 position, the screens of both pilots are controlled by the panel on the side of the first officer. The use of this system in either of BOTH's two options, makes both pilots observe the same configuration on their screens. Below is an example:

In the following example, the switch is in the normal position, that is, each control panel works with the screens of its sector.

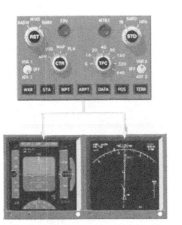

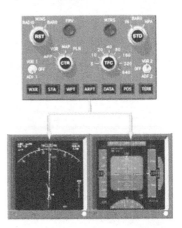

On the other hand, when the switch is in the BOTH ON 2 position, control panel 2 works with all the screens.

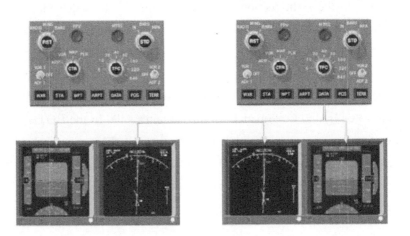

The aircraft has two "EFIS control panels" installed, one for each pilot, both have the same function and the same characteristics. They are located in the glareshield, just above the main flight screens.

Starting from left to right, point number one represents the MINS or "Minimums Reference Selector" option. It is a rotating knob that allows you to select the altitude of the minimums indicated by a procedure. This value can be selected based on the radio altimeter (RADIO) or based on the barometric altimeter (BARO).

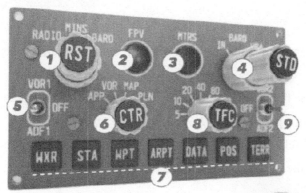

Point number two activates the option to display the "flight path vector" symbol in the attitude indicator, in addition to the "flight director" information.

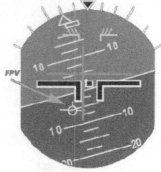

Point number three offers the possibility of changing the measurement units from feet to meters and this information is represented with a value followed by the letter M to remind the pilot that he is reading meters and not feet.

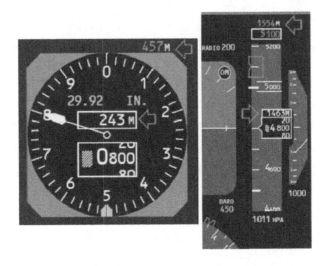

On the right margin, at point number four, the barometric reference selector is represented. It is a rotating knob where the pilot can choose the unit to use (IN or HPA), select the desired value or select the standard pressure (STD). On the sides, at points 5 and 9, there is a radio aid selection knob. On the left side, the VOR 1 and the ADF 1, while on the right side, the VOR 2 and the ADF 2.

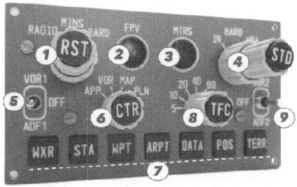

Points six and eight represent one of the most important tools on the panel. From the rotating knob of point number 6, the pilot can select the view mode he wants to observe on his Inboard display, while with knob number eight, he can select the distance range that this view can offer him. The view options offered by the system are:

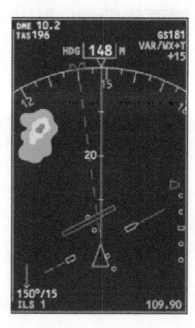

The APP approach view shows the map and the trajectory to fly along with the LOC and GS information.

The view of VOR offers a traditional HSI.

The MAP view that offers a map of the sector to fly considering keeping the flight track always up or in front.

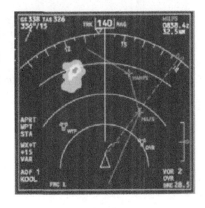

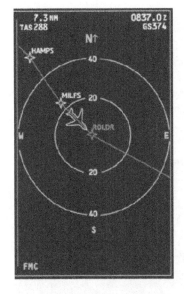

The PLN flight plan view, which offers a flat view of the aircraft being able to travel through all the points planned to fly in the flight plan just by selecting them in the FMC system.

Finally, the buttons at point number seven offer the possibility of adding visual symbols to the presentation of the selected screen. From left to right: weather radar information (WXR), radio stations (STA), waypoint (WPT), airports (ARPT), additional information to each point (DATA), position concerning references and direction to a VOR station (POS), and finally, proximity to the terrain alert information (TERR).

The primary flight screens are those mentioned as Outboard and Inboard displays, two for each pilot. These screens represent all speed information, altitudes or flight levels, headings, courses, vertical speed, flight modes, ILS system information, navigation information, and other data depending on the configuration selected by the pilot.

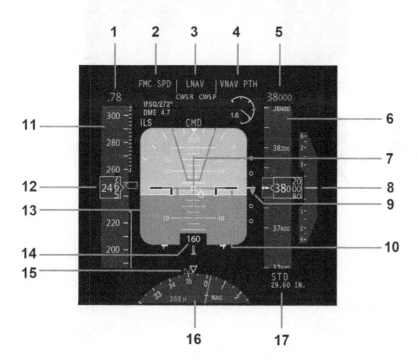

1. Air speed expressed in Mach number.

2. Parameter control by FMC (flight management computer).

3. Flight mode. Automatic side navigation activated.

4. Flight mode. Automatic vertical navigation activated.

5. Final altitude selected.

6. Altimetric scale.

7. Horizontal bar of the flight director bar.

8. Current altitude information window.

9. ILS glide slope (ILS GS) reference symbol.

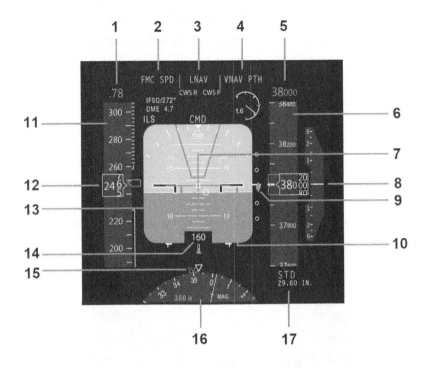

10. Visual reference symbol of the aircraft with respect to the horizon.

11. Speed scale in knots or KT (knots).

12. Current speed.

13. Flight director bar.Flight director bar

14. AGL above ground level. indicator.

15. Visual indicator of the selected course.

16. Current magnetic heading.

17. Altimetric configuration.

As mentioned above, the inboard display offers different view modes that can be selected from the EFIS system control, opting for the mode and distance range of a certain view. In the views, different visual symbols help the pilot obtain the information quickly.

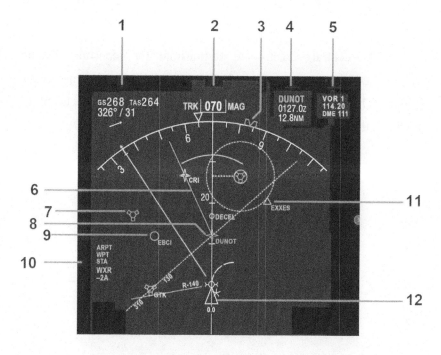

1. GS and TAS speed information and wind direction and intensity information.
2. Current route of the aircraft.
3. Selected route to follow by autopilot.
4. Information on the next point. Name, distance and expected time.
5. Information about the selected VOR. Frequency and distance.
6. Track or route of the flight plan loaded into the system.
7. VOR station en route.
8. Symbol of the next waypoint.
9. Airport symbol on the route.
10. Vital symbols added to the view from the EFIS control.
11. Waypoint en route.

12. Current position of the aircraft. This symbol is fixed and always remains in the same place, giving the possibility of the view mode to rotate around it.

The central screens are responsible for reporting on the performance of the engines, aircraft systems and failures that may occur in flight. They are divided into two, the top screen or "Upper Display" and the bottom screen or "Lower Display".

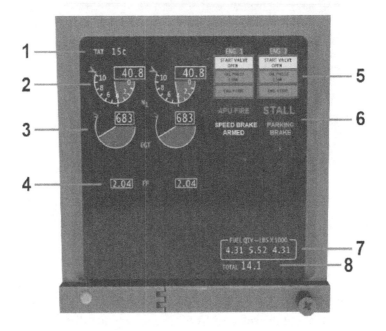

1. Total temperature value (Total Air Temperature).
2. N1 value of each engine.
3. EGT value of each engine.
4. Fuel flow value of each engine, expressed of 1,000.
5. Indicators and alerts of each engine.
6. General indicators and alerts.

7. Quantity of fuel in each tank.

8. Total fuel quantity.

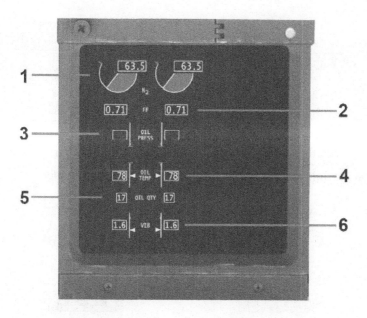

1. N2 values of each engine

2. Fuel flow values of each engine (idem to the previous one).

3. Oil pressure values of each engine.

4. Oil temperature values of each engine.

5. Oil quantity values of each engine.

6. Vibration values of each engine in scale from 1.0 to 4.0.

Communications System

The aircraft's communications system is composed of a triplicate system. The main system is on the captain's side, an additional system is on the first officer's side and a third auxiliary system is on the top panel. This third communication system can be used by an observer pilot, or as a backup system in the event of a failure of either of the two main ones. Each communication system is divided into two control

 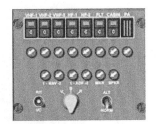

The three RTPs are located in the lower panel along with two of the ACP while the third ACP is located in the overhead panel.

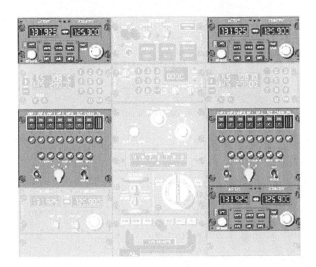

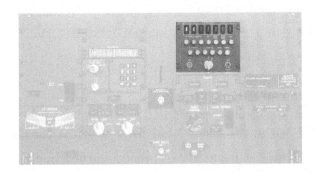

Radio Tuning Panel (RTP): from this panel, the pilot can select the frequency he wants to operate. It has the possibility of selecting three VHF systems and two HF systems, adding to the possibility of selecting a frequency in modulated amplitude or AM.

Audio Control Panel (ACP): From this panel, the pilot can select the frequency at which he wants to listen or transmit and adjust the volume of the sound. Additionally, the connection function with the communication system of oxygen masks is added.

In case of any degradation of the communications system, the GPA would be inoperative. Considering this possibility, it has a function in an alternative mode, where the entire ACP remains inoperative and only one radio is enabled. In the captain's ACP, VHF 1. In the ACP of the first officer, VHF 2. And in the ACP support, VHF 3. This function is activated from the knob in the lower right margin of the ACP, taking it from the NORM (normal) position to the ALT (alternative) position.

In the lower central part of the ACP is a knob with three positions: V (Voice), receives the voices of the frequencies of NAV and ADF. B (both), receives the voices of the NAV and ADF frequencies along with the audio identifier of each station. R (Range), receives the sound of the identifier of each station.

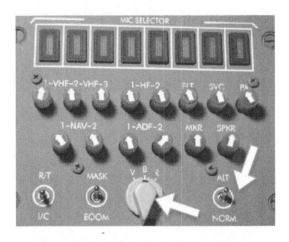

Recording System,

The aircraft recording system is divided into two parts. A flight data recorder system and a voice recording system in the cockpit (cockpit voice recorder). The flight data recording system collects information throughout the operation from the moment the plane is energized until the engines stop. The cabin voice recording system uses the same operating principle but stops when the plane runs out of power. This cabin voice recording system not only records the voices of the cockpit, but also the communications that the pilot makes from the selection at the ACP. The voice recording extends for 120 minutes continuously, then it is automatically deleted and the recording cycle is restarted for another 120 minutes. Both control panels of the recording systems are located in the upper panel. The flight data recording panel is on the upper rear panel and the cockpit voice recording panel is on the upper centre panel.

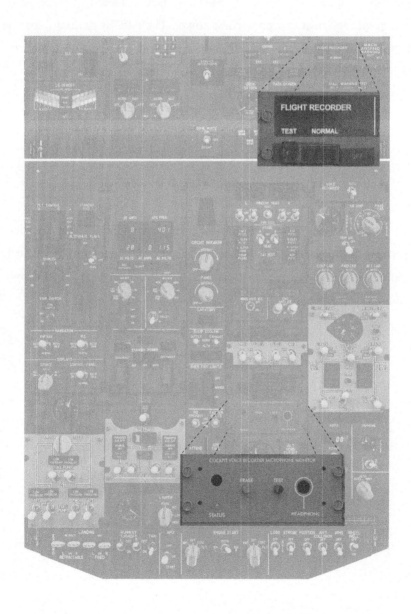

APU (Auxiliar Power Unit)

The "auxiliary power unit" or APU, is located in the tail cone of the aircraft and can supply the electrical and pneumatic system of the aircraft if necessary. For this reason, it is considered an alternative source of electrical and pneumatic power. The APU is nothing more or less than a turbine, an engine, and as such, it needs to be turned on manually. To do this, there are three sources of power, capable of turning the APU on. They are:

- An external power source or GPU (ground power unit).
- The batteries of the plane.
- And the same plane, once turned on, at least one of its engines.

The APU can generate electrical energy to supply all the electrical systems of the aircraft, when it has its motors and generators turned off. Moreover, it also has the ability to generate pneumatic power to supply all the systems that require it.

The APU can be turned on and operated up to the maximum flight altitude certified by the aircraft. It is supplied with fuel from the left tank and is operated manually from the control panel located in the overhead panel.

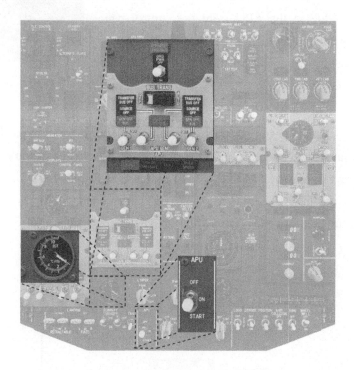

When the APU switch is in the OFF position, the system is turned off, except in the situation in which the APU has been used and recently turned off by the pilot, a situation in which the APU will remain on for 60 more seconds as part of the cooling process, even if the switch is OFF. When the switch is in the START position, the power cycle starts, and at the end of this, the pilot turns the switch to the ON position indicating that the system will remain on.

The operation of the APU is controlled by a control electronics unit called ECU (electronic control unit). When the ECU detects a significant variation in any of the APU's engine parameters, it proceeds to an automatic shutdown. The pilot can verify the EGT value of the APU from the control panel that provides an analog temperature indicator, just below the panel where the APU generator switches are.

This option is located in the generator panel next to the generator switch of each motor and the activation switch of the external power equipment or "GPU". At the bottom of this panel are four visual alerts of the APU system. A MAINT maintenance alert, a low oil pressure alert, a system failure alert and an over speed alert.

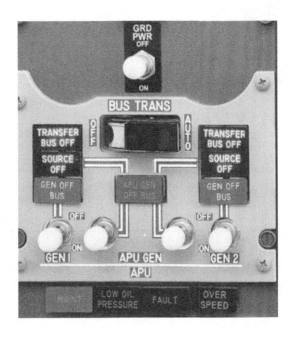

As in engines, the APU has a firefighting system in case the internal engine is affected by such a situation. This system offers two warnings, one on board inside the cockpit and another outside the fuselage to inform ground personnel about this situation.

Outside, a warning light is lit on the APU operating panel, indicating to ground personnel that there is a fire event and that they must act immediately.

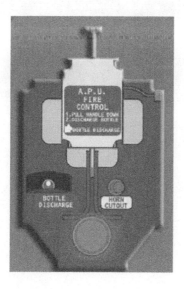

Inside the flight deck, the FIRE WARM audio visual alarm is activated on both sides of the fault panel.

Along with this, the light indication of the fire protection panel is activated in the APU section, indicating that there is a fire in the system. From this panel, the pilot will be able to activate the fire extension system. The fire protection panel is located just below the acceleration quadrant of the engines and includes the firefighting system for both engines.

Systems II

B737-700/800/900

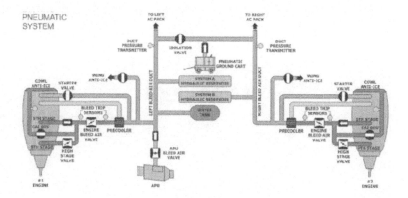

NOTE: information not valid for real flights. For this purpose, refer to the manufacturer's original manuals.

Fuel System

The fuel system of the B737 has three tanks. A central tank, and two side tanks named tank 1 (left) and tank 2 (right). In total, the aircraft has a load capacity of 20,896 kilograms of fuel, distributed as follows:

TANK	GALLONS	POUNDS*	LITERS	KILOGRAMS*
NO. 1	1,288	8,630	4,876	3,915
NO. 2	1,288	8,630	4,876	3,915
CENTER	4,299	28,803	16,273	13,066
TOTAL	6,875	46,063	26,025	20,896

Main tanks 1 and 2, are located within the wing structure, while the central tank is below the fuselage structure. Each tank uses two electric pumps that direct the fuel towards the engines, and with the passage of this through the ducts, the pumps are cooled and lubricated.

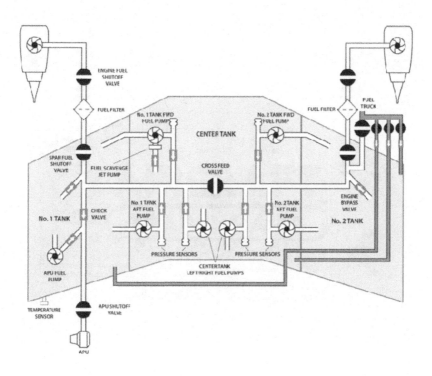

The electric pumps of the central tank generate high pressure, much higher than the pumps of the main tanks. As a result, the fuel of the central tank will be used in the first instance, even if the pumps of the main tanks are operational and working.

Above the central duct is a fuel cross-feed valve known as "Cross Feed" or "X-Feed". This valve allows one engine to feed on the fuel of the opposite wing, that is, with the fuel that also feeds the other engine. This specific procedure is used in case there is an imbalance of fuel between the wings or there is an engine failure and it is planned to use the fuel of that engine in the other. The procedure is simple, the centre pumps and the engine to which you want to supply are deactivated, the X-Feed is opened and the pressure of the engine pump that supplies it will take the fuel to the other side passing through the open X-Feed.

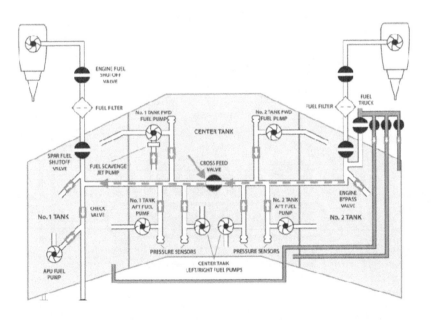

The fuel path begins from the pump of each tank and travels through the ducts until it reaches the first shutoff valve, before entering the engine. From there, it reaches a first instance fuel pump, which allows the flow to increase its pressure and follows its path towards a fuel filter that will remove contaminants to take the fuel to a second instance pump. This second pump increases the fuel pressure again to direct it to a hydromechanical unit or HMU, where the electronic engine control or EEC will pass the fuel required for the selected power.

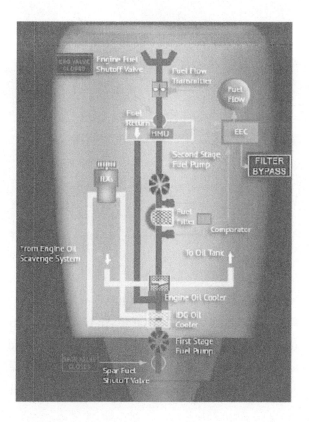

The fuel panel is located above the top panel or overhead panel. From there, the pilot can operate the fuel pumps and the cross-feed valve or X-Feed.

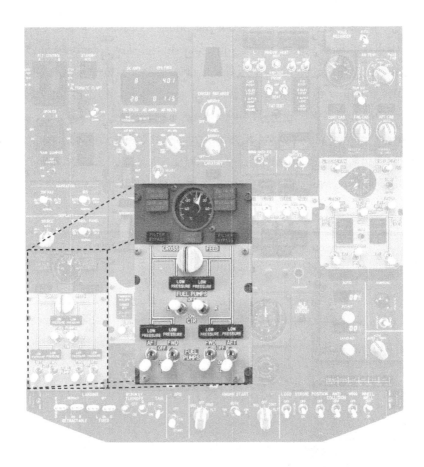

The fuel panel is composed of two knobs in each pump that allow them to be selected in ON or OFF. Above each pump, the "low pressure" light indicators are located. The panel has a rotating knob to open or close the cross-feed valve and an analog fuel temperature indicator. It also has closed valve light indicators and a fuel filter.

Fuel indications are presented in the Upper Display Unit (DU), located in the main panel and offer different view options depending on the model and operator's choice.

The information is located on the lower right margin of the DU (the location could vary depending on the models) and may present various options of views and units of measurement:

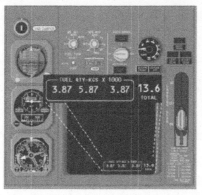

The fuel flow pressure indication presents the same variables as the fuel quantity indication. Add a visual low-pressure alert indication on the indicator of each tank.

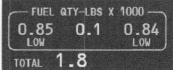

In case the system detects an imbalance of 1000 LBS or higher in the fuel quantities of the tanks, it will issue a visual alert similar to the previous one but with the word IMBAL (imbalance) about the information of the affected tank.

Electrical System

The aircraft is equipped with an electrical system composed of three generators, one in each engine, and one in the APU. Additionally, it offers the possibility of connecting a fourth external generator or GPU (ground power unit).

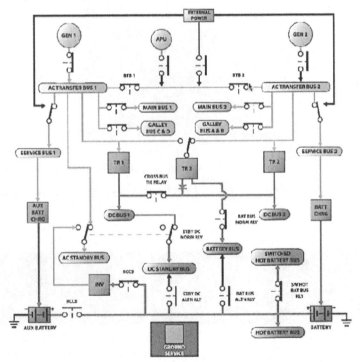

The work of the electrical system begins in the generators. These generators maintain a constant speed due to the work of a mechanism known as IDG (intregrated drive generator).

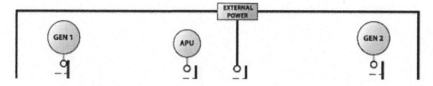

Each generator supplies alternate current to its own current transfer bar. That is, generator one supplies transfer bar (bus) one and generator two to transfer bar (bus) two.

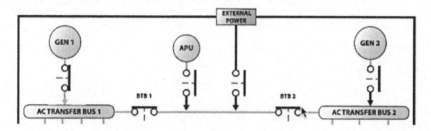

From these transfer bars, alternating current is sent to different areas depending on each requirement. Part of this current flow continues its journey to a set of three transformers that convert it into direct current or DC (Direct current).

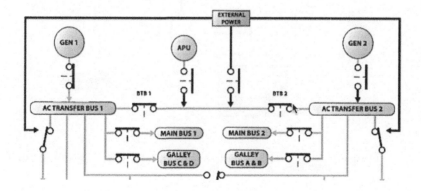

Transformer 1 receives the alternating current of transfer bar 1 and transformer 2, of transfer bar 2. For its part, transformer 3, receives alternating current from transfer bar 2, but if bar 2 is inoperative, transformer 3, will receive alternating current from transfer bar 1.

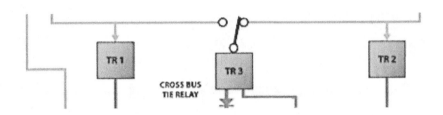

After the current conversion process, the transformers send direct current or DC to three zones, direct current bar 1 or DC BUS 1, direct current bar 2 or DC BUS 2 and direct current bar in standby or DC STBY BUS.

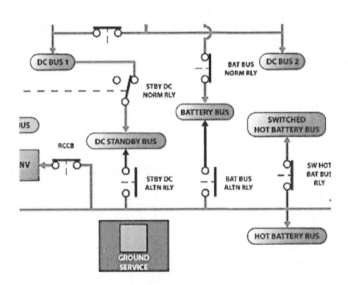

Observing the current flow diagram, it is observed that transformer 3 supplies the battery power bar.

Analysing the complete graph again, the current flow path starts from the generators, travels to the AC or AC current transfer bars. From there, it goes to different areas as required, and part of this current flow continues its journey to the transformers, where it passes from AC to DC. Each transformer takes power from its own transfer bar, except transformer number three that takes power from transfer bar number two. From the main transformers (1 and 2), the direct current is directed towards DC BUS 1 and DC BUS2 bars, while the direct current of transformer three, is directed towards the battery bar or BATTERY BUS.

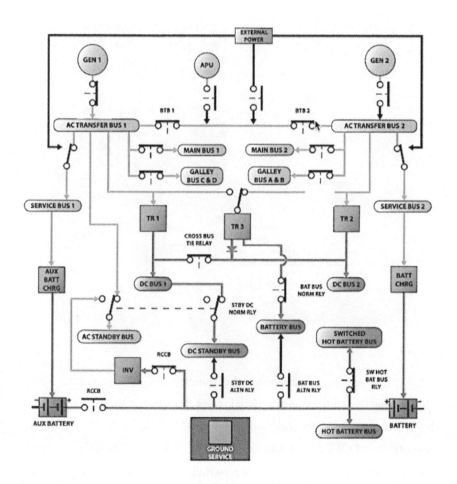

The electrical system is controlled from its panel located in the overhead panel. Hence, the pilot can control the generators, the battery, the passage of AC alternating current and DC direct current, the APU generator, the transfer bar, the auxiliary power unit (GPU) and a complete voltage test of each section.

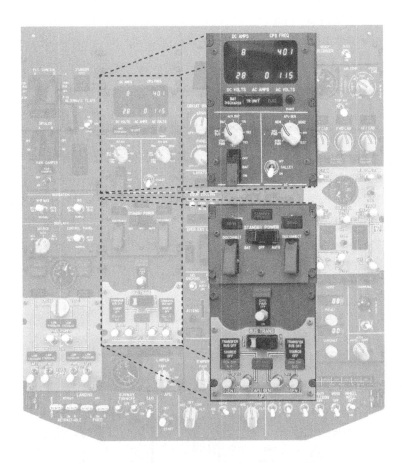

In the lower section are the switches for each generator with their respective indications or visual alerts. In between these, the transfer bar operation   offers two positions: AUTO for a fully automatic operation and OFF to disable or isolate AC TRANSFER BUS 1 of AC TRANSFER BUS 2. Above is the switch to activate or deactivate the

GPU (Ground Power Unit) along with a visual alert that tells the pilot when the GPU is available. The panel continues with a security section. Two switches that disable the IDGs are protected with a red safety cover to prevent their involuntary operation. From these switches, the pilot can disconnect the IDG of each generator. Normally, when a switch is protected with a security guard, confirmation from both pilots is required for its operation. In between these switches, the operation switch of the power source is located in standby and above it, three visual indications or alerts, one for each IDG and the central one for the standby.

At the top is a control panel of the electrical system and its derivatives. It has a main screen and three indicators or visual alerts. From the left sector, the pilot can take the measurement of the battery, transformers and current in standby, selecting the system he wants with the rotating knob. Underneath it, there is a switch to activate or deactivate the battery. From the right side, the pilot can take the measurement of the generators of each engine, the APU generator and perform a generalized test. Below, there is a switch that activates the current in the area of the Galley or island to this sector in case of any failure.

Hydraulic System (Hydra)

The aircraft is equipped with three hydraulic systems, a system A, a system B and a third standby system in case the pressure of system A or B drops to such an extent that it affects other systems. The hydraulic system supplies the following systems:

Flight controls. Flaps and Slats Undercarriage

Brake Systems   Nose Wheel Steering Wheel

Automatic pilot Reversers.

Hydraulic systems A and B are pressurized by the pneumatic system, while the third hydraulic system is connected to hydraulic system B for pressurization. Each hydraulic system has two pumps, one mechanical connected with the engine on the system side, and one electric. The system as a whole has a transfer unit known as the PTU (power transfer unit), which works similarly to the X-Feed of the fuel system.

When hydraulic system B detects low fluid pressure, the OCT is activated and transfers pressure fluid from system A to compensate for the pressure values in system B. Finally, it has a pressure transfer unit for the landing gear called LDTU (landing gear transfer unit) and is used to retract the landing gear when the hydraulic pressure of system A is not enough or below the minimum value. In this case, the LDTU is activated and pressure is taken from system B to compensate for the value of A.

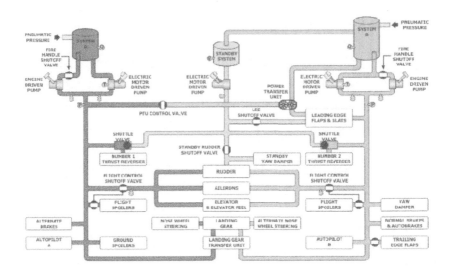

The reservoirs of each hydraulic system are located in the centre of the aircraft and have a cylindrical shape connected to the respective hoses or hydraulic ducts.

Each hydraulic system has a certain role in each of the remaining systems. The following table shows the systems and devices that work with each of the hydraulic systems.

System A	System B	Standby System
Rudder	Rudder	STBY Yaw Damper
Ailerons	Ailerons	STBY Rudder PCU
Elevator and Elevator Feel	Elevator and Elevator Feel	Autoslats
#1 Thrust Reverser	#2 Thrust Reverser	and
Flight Spoilers	Autoslats	Leading Edge Flaps/Slats
Ground Spoilers	and	#1 Thrust Reverser
Landing Gear	Leading Edge Flaps/Slats	#2 Thrust Reverser
Nosewheel Steering	Flight Spoilers	
Alternate Brakes	Landing Gear Transfer Unit	
Autopilot A	Alternate NWS	
Main Cargo Door	Normal Brakes	
Power Transfer Unit	Autopilot B	
	Yaw Damper	
	Trailing Edge Flaps	

The control panel of the hydraulic system is located in the centre of the overhead panel and has 4 activation knobs for the hydraulic pumps of each system.

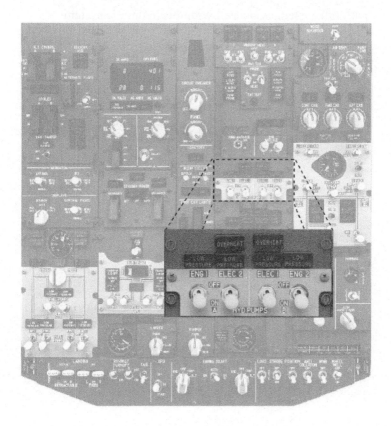

At its top it has 6 light indicators, three for each system, which report anomalies such as low pressure or overheating.

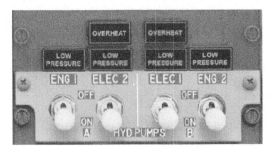

For its part, the third hydraulic system has a separate panel from the main one mentioned above. This is because its activation is optional and depends on the requirements of the pilots to operate a certain aircraft system associated with this hydraulic system.

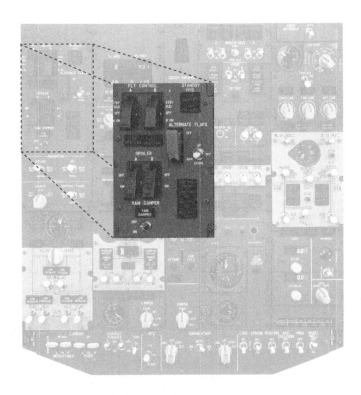

Landing Train System,

The aircraft is equipped with a retractable landing gear system. This system is composed of a main train with two groups of two wheels located under the wings and near the fuselage; and a nose train composed of a single group of two wheels located just below the cockpit.

The retraction of the main train is inside the fuselage while the retraction of the nose train is forward, entering its compartment just below the cabin.

On the ground, the wheels of the landing gear direct the aircraft during the running, takeoff and landing procedure. From the cockpit, pilots control the direction of the nose train with the pedals located under the main panel inside the cockpit. The pedals are used for small changes in the direction of the aircraft, since they limit their radius of action to a maximum of 7° of rotation for taxiing, takeoff and landing maneuvers.

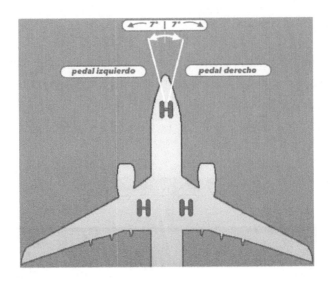

The control of the pedals on the nose wheel is associated, in most cases, with takeoff and landing procedures, due to their reduced angle of operation. When the pilot needs to increase the radius of action of the nose wheel during taxiing operations, he uses the nose wheel addressing system known as "Nose Wheel Steering". The NWS system is operated from the cockpit by a semicircle-shaped rotating lever.

When the pilot drives the lever of the NWS system, it can achieve up to a maximum of 78° turning radius during taxiing operations. This value offers the possibility of turning the aircraft at an almost right angle..

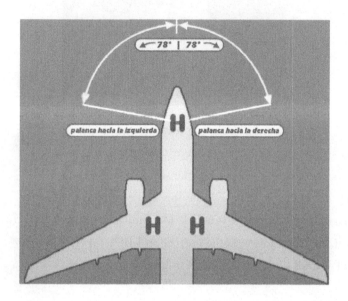

Both the NWS system and the complete operation of the landing gear are operated by the hydraulic system "A" during a normal operation. In case of low pressure of the hydraulic system "A", the landing gear transfer unit is activated, transferring hydraulic pressure from the "B" system to ensure the operation of the landing gear.

The landing gear control panel is located in the main panel, to the right of the upper display. It is composed of a system drive lever with three available positions and three visual alerts that warn the pilot about the status of the system operation.

When the pilot takes the lever to the down or DN position, the hydraulic system "A" generates the pressure necessary to unlock the train system and extend it in its entirety. When the three groups of wheels of the train are extended, the indicator lights warn of this situation with the indication LEFT GEAR, RIGHT GEAR and NOSE GEAR in green.

After takeoff, the pilot takes the landing gear lever to the UP position. This action causes the system to start the retraction of the train through the hydraulic pressure of the "A" system. In this instance, the system slows the movement of the train wheels automatically by taking the three groups of wheels to their respective compartments. From here, the indicator lights change to red indicating that the train is in transit. When your route ends, the signs will turn off completely.

Once the train retraction has finished, the pilot takes the lever to the OFF position. This will cause the hydraulic pressure to be removed from the system and the locks or obstacles are activated to avoid involuntary actions.

In addition to the light signals or indications of the system drive, on the overhead panel there is this same information with the same operating principle in order to offer redundancy in the information.

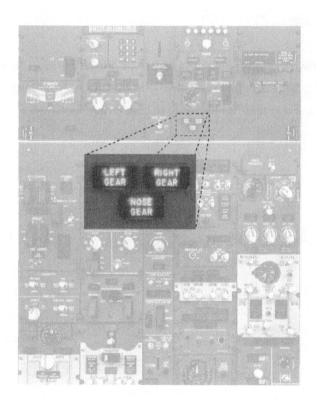

The landing gear braking system is composed of normal braking and alternative braking. Normal braking uses the hydraulic pressure of system B, while alternative braking uses the hydraulic pressure of system A.

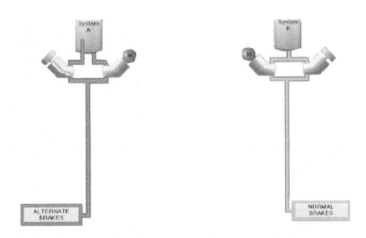

The system offers a third source of pressure in case the first two fail or are not enough. From hydraulic system B, a braking pressure accumulator is extended to be used in case of emergency.

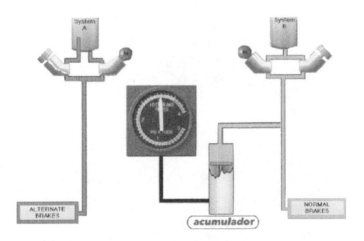

The braking accumulator indicator is located in the main panel, just above the inboard display of the first officer.

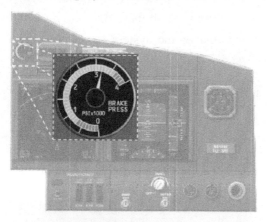

As part of the standard equipment of the braking system, the aircraft has an additional automatic braking system known as AUTOBRAKE, used to brake automatically during an aborted takeoff and during the landing run. The AUTOBRAKE system has five levels of intensity, 1, 2, 3, maximum and RTO (rejected takeoff). Its operation is given by hydraulic system B, only in normal braking mode.

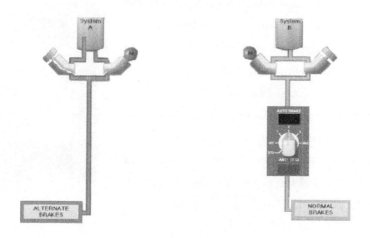

This system is activated manually from the control panel located above the main panel, just above the upper display. This control panel consists of a rotating knob that offers the possibility of selecting the modes of operation of the system or deactivating it in the OFF position.

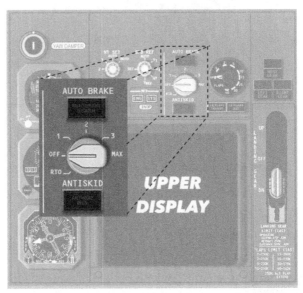

During an aborted takeoff (RTO), the activation of the autobrake system occurs when the aircraft exceeds 90 kt of speed and the accelerators are located in the idle position. This will activate automatic braking at its maximum capacity. During the landing run, the autobrake system is activated when the main train exerts pressure with the surface of the runway and the accelerators are located in the idle position.

In case the pilot deactivates the autobrake during the operation, the panel indicator will announce this condition with a light signal.

The final variant of the braking system is the parking brake or "Parking Brake". This system can be activated from both pilot stations. Its activation is a joint work between the pedal brake and the system activation lever, located on the acceleration quadrant.

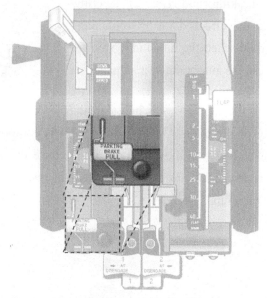

To activate the system, the pilot must press and maintain the pedals in order to generate a certain braking pressure, and then adjust the system lever to its activation position. This will cause a red light to turn on indicating that the system is activated.

As an additional function to the braking system, the anti-skid function is added on the train wheels when braking the aircraft. It is an automatic system that prevents unwanted sliding of the train wheels, blocking these during braking and loss of steering control due to the effects of a hydroplaning. Pilots are warned when the antiskid system is inoperative from the autobrake system panel.

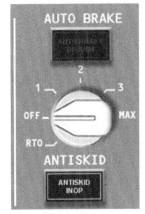

Finally, the landing gear has a manual extension function in case of failure of the main system. This system is composed of three manual extension levers of the landing gear, one for each set of wheels. This section is located at the back of the cabin, just behind the first officer's position on the ground.

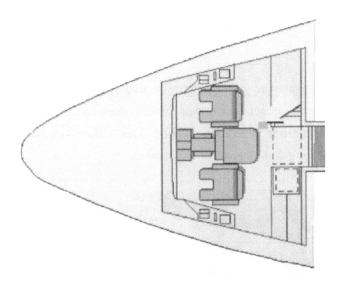

When lifting the lid that covers the panel, the pilot encounters three red levers, one for each part of the train.

The procedure consists of three steps. In the first instance, the pilot must bring the landing gear lever to the OFF position. After that, pull each of the manual activation levers until all the wheels of the train are down. Finally, the pilot must bring the train lever to the DN (down) position so that the system locks and secures the train wheels for safe operation.

Pneumatic System

The air supplyed the pneumatic system can be obtained from three different sources: from the engines, from the APU, or from an external pneumatic source. Both the APU and the external source provide air flow to the ducts before the ignition of the engines. Once the engines are already running, they are in charge of supplying the pneumatic system. Systems based on the pneumatic system are:

1. Air-conditioning

2. Pressurization

3. Anti-ice system

4. Engine ignition

5. Pressurization of hydraulic containers and water tank

The pneumatic system develops an airflow system that serves as a power supply to the aforementioned items. This system is known as "Bleed Air System". The pneumatic system diagram offers different valves and ducts through which the air flow travels to and from the engines, passing through different stages to supply the rest of the systems that require it.

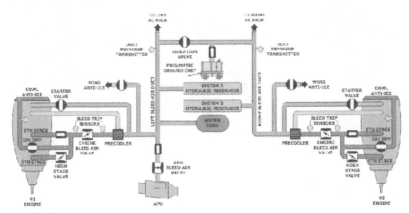

The engine airflow system or "Engine Bleed Air" is supplied with air from the fifth and ninth sections of the engine compressor. When the air obtained from the fifth section of the compressor has enough pressure for the operation, it will no longer be necessary to take more air from the next section. In order to maintain a correct airflow with adequate pressure, there are the airflow valves of each engine known as "Engine Bleed Valve". Between the systems of each engine, there is an isolation valve that keeps both airflow systems separate from each other. The isolation valve is activated when one of the engine bleed air systems is in failure or is turned off, in order to supply the entire pneumatic system with the remaining system. For its part, the APU also has an airflow system and a regulation valve. This system is known as APU Bleed Air and its APU Bleed Air Valve. The entire Bleed system assembly is operated from the control panel located in the overhead panel.

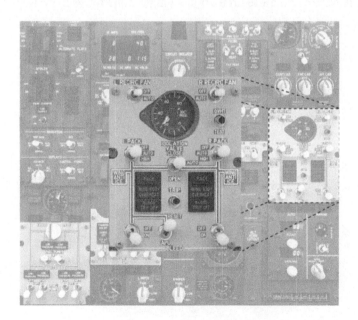

Starting from the bottom of the panel, the three knobs operating the Air Bleed systems are located, one for each engine and one for the APU system. Continuing with the guide lines upwards, the panel reaches the switches of the air conditioning packs, one for each Engine Bleed Air, and in between these, the knob selected by the Isolation Valve.

Between the switches, in the central part of the panel, there are six light warnings, three for each system. These indications warn of three possible situations. An excess temperature in the air conditioning pack system, an overheating in the air ducts or, an excess temperature or pressure in the Engine Bleed Air system on the warned side. At the top is a pressure indicator in the air ducts, reporting a value with two needles, one with the letter L for the left system and another with the letter R for the right system. Finally, at the top, on the right and left side, there are two air recirculation switches, one for each system.

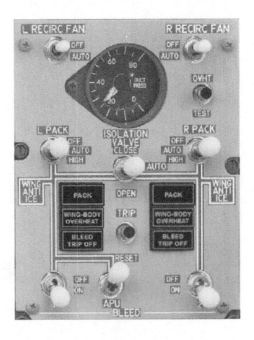

The air conditioning system is manually regulated by the pilots from the cockpit. The hot air that comes from the engines regulates its passage into the ducts by means of an engine bleed valve and goes through a precooler process that regulates its temperature according to what the pilot has selected from the control panel. This airflow travels through the ducts until it reaches the air conditioning packs, one for each engine (left pack and right pack), then located in a unit called Mix Manifold, and from there, head towards one of the three temperature zones of the plane.

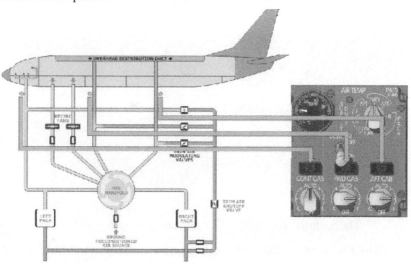

The aircraft has three temperature zones, the cockpit, and the separate passenger cabin in front and rear sectors.This distribution allows independent air conditioning between the zones and each temperature is regulated from the control panel located in the overhead panel.

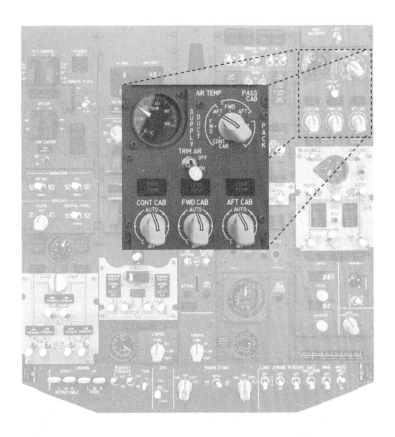

The control panel has three rotating knobs, one for each air conditioning area. When turning the knob, the pilot regulates the temperature of the desired area. The temperature range ranges from 18°C to 30°C. Optionally you can operate the system automatically by taking the knob to the AUTO position. Above each knob is a visual warning indicator that lights up and displays the ZONE TEMP message when the area has an excess temperature or when a system failure associated with this area is detected.

In the centre of the panel is the valve activation key that regulates the amount of air flowing through the ducts. In the upper left there is a temperature indicator for each zone and to its right, the selector of the area you want to rate the temperature.

Cabin pressurization is controlled throughout the flight by the CPCS or "Cabin Pressure Control System". This system has two automatic control channels (AUTO and ALTN) and a manual control mode (MAN) operated by the pilot from the control panel located in the overhead panel. The system uses the air flow from the air conditioning system and is controlled by a valve that regulates the external flow, known as "Outflow Valve". It has two pressure relief valves that limit the internal and outer differential pressure to a maximum of 9.1 psi.

Cabin Pressure Controller (CPC) is located in the upper panel and allows controlling the simulated altitude of the cabin up to a value of 8,000 feet for maximum flights on an aircraft operating roof of 41,000 feet. This control panel consists of a rotating knob to select the mode of operation of the system. It is a manual operation knob of the "Outflow" valve allowing the pilot to open or close it depending on the need for pressurization when the system is operating in manual mode and a visual indicator of the position of this valve just above the knob. On the left side it has two windows and two rotating knobs to select the flight altitude (upper window) and to select the elevation of the destination aerodrome (lower window), all in case the system is operated manually.

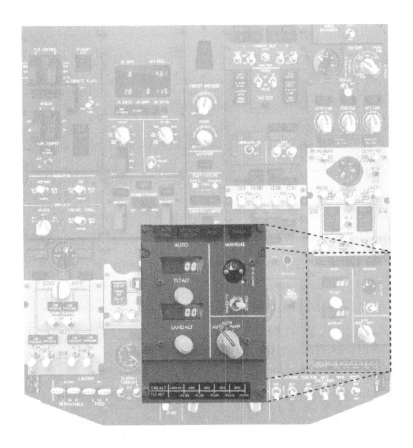

At the top of the panel are four visual alerts that are illuminated in each case.

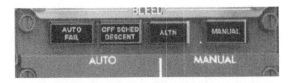

At the bottom is added a reference table of the recommended cabin altitudes for each actual flight altitude.

The final scheme of the pressurization system is diagrammed as follows:

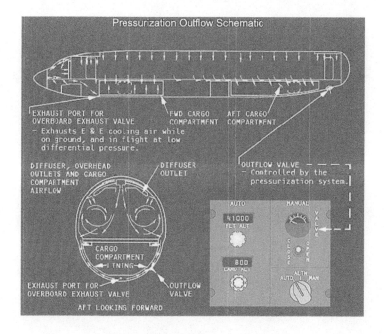

For operations where it is planned to land at high elevation airports, there is a special pressurization system, which, when activated manually by the pilot, decreases the cabin altitude to the elevation of the airport while the aircraft is in descent mode. This system presents its control panel in the overhead panel, to the left of the CPC panel.

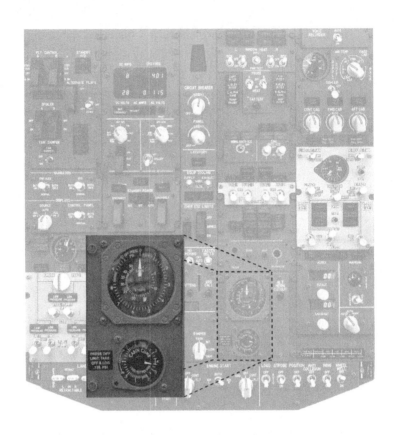

Systems III

B737-700/800/900

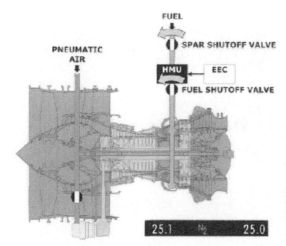

FUEL

SPAR SHUTOFF VALVE

PNEUMATIC AIR

HMU ← EEC

FUEL SHUTOFF VALVE

25.1   N₂   25.0

**START LEVERS
ADVANCED
TO IDLE**

Power Plant

The aircraft is equipped with two double rotor CFM56-7 engines that deliver a maximum power of 27,300 lbs.

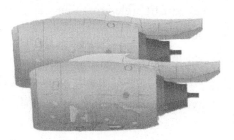

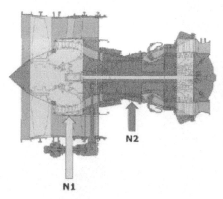

Each engine is composed of a series of parts that form the power plant. Among the main components are two rotors (N1 and N2) mechanically independent of each other.

The first N1 rotor consists of three working sections. The initial FAN, composed of a series of wheel-shaped blades, a low-pressure compressor and a low-pressure turbine.

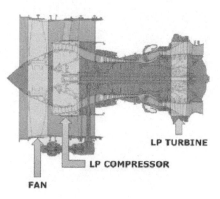

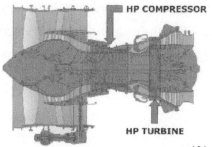

The second N2 rotor consists of two sections. A high-pressure compressor and a high-pressure turbine.

Each engine is regulated by a double electronic control channel called EEC (electronic engine control). Its operating principle is based on the information received from the AUTO THROTTLE system and the location of the accelerator levers. With this information, the EEC system regulates the amount of fuel that reaches the engine, through a hydromechanical unit called HMU (hydro mechanic unit).

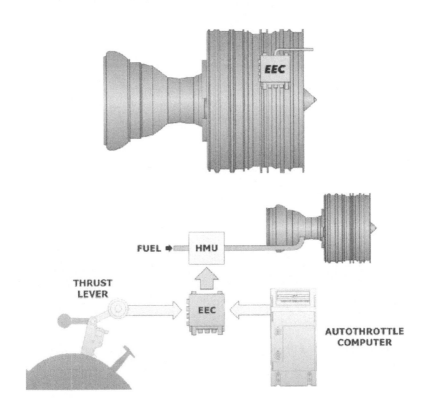

The operating principle of this engine is similar to the rest of the aeronautical jet engines. It is based on the path of the air that enters the engine and crosses different stages until it generates the ignition that gives rise to power.

The air flow enters the engine through the FAN from the front section. After crossing the FAN, the air takes two different paths. A proportion of the air mass travels through the center of the engine, passing through the compressor section and the combustion chamber, where it will be mixed with the fuel to generate the ignition that will lead to traction. This air travel is called primary airflow and provides approximately 80% of the engine's power. The remaining airflow, known as secondary airflow, runs through the edges of the engine until it is expelled from the rear.

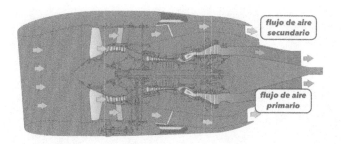

Part of the secondary air flow gives function to the reverser system. This system is based on opening the internal cavity of the engine to allow the secondary air flow to leave, generating a reverse thrust to the traction, which reduces the action it exerts on the landing run or during the run of an aborted takeoff (RTO)

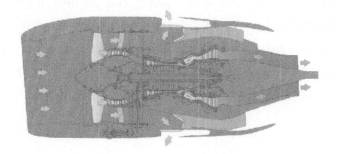

The principle of operation of the engine is based on a series of subsystems located within the engine system. These subsystems work together to ensure successful operation. Within each N2 rotor are located the fuel, oil and hydraulic pumps, along with the AC electric generator, all contained in a section known as "Gearbox". The operation of these subsystems is indispensable for the correct operation of the engine. The principle of operation of each one is detailed below.

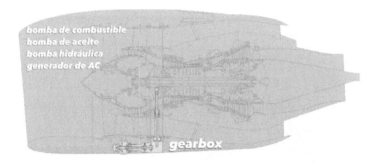

The fuel goes through a series of stages until it reaches the combustion chamber of the engine. This tour is possible by the work of the fuel pump that guarantees a pressure on its flow. Fuel from tanks passes through the first instance pump, increases its pressure to pass through temperature exchange devices until it reaches the filter, where it will eliminate all contaminants. When leaving the filter, it goes through the second instance pump to recover the pressure lost in the previous stages until it reaches the HMU, where the fuel flow will be regulated by this system considering the operation of the EEC, from there to the last instance, the fuel flow transmitter and then to the engine.

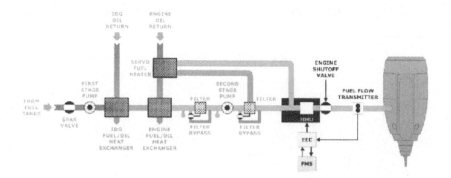

Between the HMU unit and the fuel flow transmitter, the engine shut-off valve is located. When this valve is closed, the fuel will not reach the combustion chamber and the engine will stop. From the cockpit, pilots observe the information coming from the "Fuel Flow Transmitter", in the DUs (Upper and Lower displays).

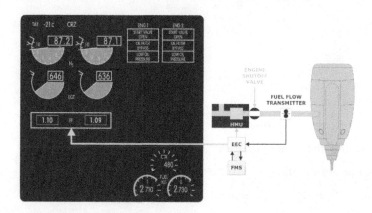

Apart from that, the oil pump performs a similar operation to the fuel pump, except that the path of this fluid is different. The oil travels from its tank to the engine-driven oil pump. From here, it acquires enough pressure to start the journey through different sections, passing through a filter that eliminates contaminants, then through an oil temperature sensor and continues its journey until it reaches the engine. Within the system, the oil fulfills two functions, to cool and lubricate the engine and its components. At the end of the cycle, the remaining oil returns to the system with a route that takes it through different instances until it reaches the beginning again to start its route again.

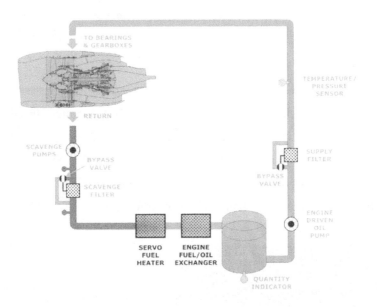

At the time of starting the engine, the system takes air pressure from three possible sources: from the other engine already on, from the APU or from an external pneumatic source.

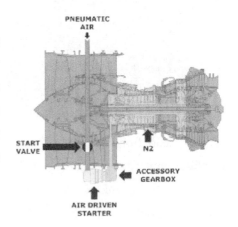

The start valve opens allowing air flow to enter. When the N2 value reaches 25%, the pilot takes the acceleration levers to the IDLE position, this will open the fuel valve and the HMU valve. This process will lead to the next step, ignition.

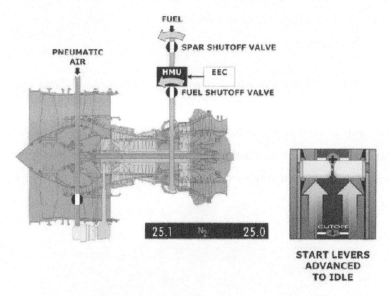

START LEVERS
ADVANCED
TO IDLE

From the bottom panel or "Pedestal Panel", the pilot can control the power of the engines and the reverse system, all from the acceleration quadrant.

Acceleration levers have a 58° travel from the IDLE position to the maximum power position. During manual power operation, the pilot will be able to adjust this value as necessary, but always within this operating range.

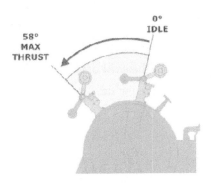

The EEC system offers two power control modes, one normal and one alternative. In normal mode, the ECC considers current flight conditions and air pressure demand to control a correct N1 value. While in alternative mode, current flight conditions are not taken into account. These power control modes have their panel located in the overhead rear panel.

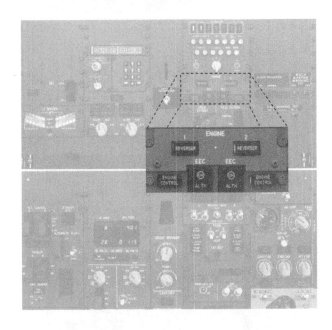

Within the same ECC panel, the two reverser indicators are located, one for each engine. The reverser system reverses the flow of power generating a push reduction action during the landing run or during an aborted takeoff.

The reverse activation levers are located in front of each acceleration lever corresponding to each engine. Its activation is backwards, in the same sense as the reduction of power.

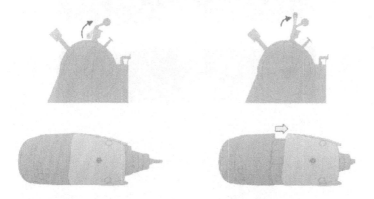

The activation of the system is subject to compliance with three conditions. The aircraft must be less than 10 feet high or already on the ground, the battery must be ON and the fire protection switches associated with each engine must be down or off. Any deviation from these three parameters would make it impossible to operate the reversers.

As additional protection to the system, the reverse lever is locked in the IDLE REV position until the system has reached 60% of the action. This will prevent the pilot from accidentally carrying the levers forward.

When the reverser system is activated, on the upper display, just above the N1 indications of each engine, the word REV appears indicating that the system has been activated. While the reversers are on the way to their full deployment, the word REV will be displayed in amber. Once the reversers are fully deployed, the word REV will be displayed in green.

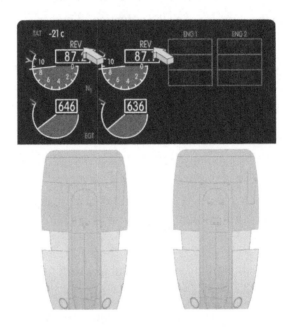

Traffic Alert and Collision Avoidance System TCAS

The aircraft has a traffic alert and collision escape system in flight. The system is a radar that identifies any aircraft within a range of action and indicates this information in the DUs. If necessary, the TCAS system indicates the steps to follow by offering instructions to evade the possible collision. The system presents the warnings and instructions on the primary displays, both on the captain's side and on the first officer's side.

In the inboard display on both sides, the TCAS system presents visual alerts of aircraft at risk of proximity collision, using the following symbology.

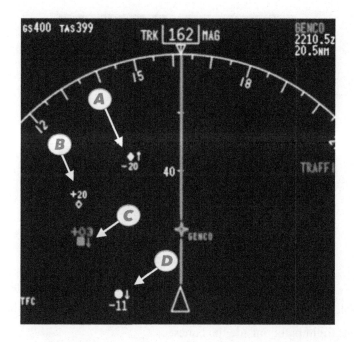

The aircraft symbol "A" indicates an up arrow informing that the aircraft is on the rise. Under the white icon, the current altitude of the aircraft is reported, in this case -20 or 2000 feet below. In example "B", the traffic detected by the TCAS, is in level flight, 2000 feet above the aircraft.

In examples "C" and "D", color coding is added in order to raise the alert level. Example C shows a red icon, reporting that the aircraft is above only 300 feet and in descent, which implies an imminent risk of collision. For its part, example D is presented in yellow, indicating a lower degree of risk than the previous example. He reports that the aircraft is in descent but already below 1100 feet.

On the outboard display on both sides, the TCAS system offers a guide for the flight path in case it is necessary to evade a possible collision with another aircraft.

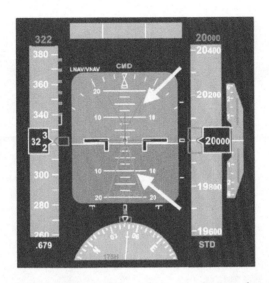

This visual reference is based on a red cone that indicates the possible collision path. Based on this reference, the aircraft should keep its own flight path, outside the cones.

The TCAS system offers two types of alerts, "Traffic Advisors (TA)" and "Resolution Advisors (RA)". On the one hand, a proximity warning between aircraft (TA), when the second aircraft is 45 seconds away in a possible collision course. On the other hand, a resolution to the previous warning (RA), when the second aircraft continues to approach and is 25 seconds from the possible collision. In this case, the TCAS system will be activated on both aircraft and will inform of the instructions to follow, opposite for each aircraft, that is, one aircraft will be given ascent instructions and the other aircraft will be given descent instructions.

The TCAS system panel is located in the bottom panel or "pedestal panel". It can present different models depending on the manufacturer, but all responding to the same operating principle. The TCAS system shares the panel with the aircraft transponder. In its upper right margin is a rotating knob that allows you to select the mode of operation of the system with two options for the TCAS, TA Only activating only the warning system without conflict resolution and TA/ RA activating the complete warning and conflict resolution system.

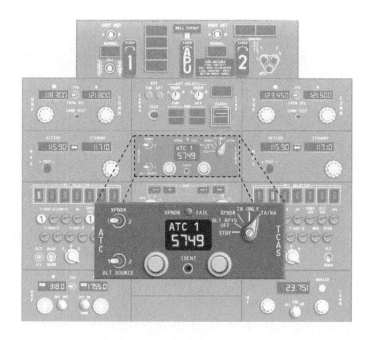

Ice and Rain protection

Most commercial aircraft have a protection system that keeps the main surfaces that are in direct contact with the atmosphere clean of rain and ice. In this case, the aircraft has a rain and ice protection system that applies to four sectors outside the aircraft: the cockpit windshield, the slat surface at the leading edge, the front surface of the engines and all the ports and sockets of the aircraft.

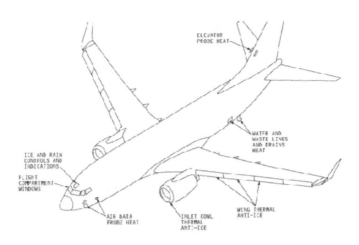

The front surface of the engines prevents the formation of ice with a hot air system from the engines that heats the entire area. The entire line of slats at the leading edge uses the hot air flow that comes from a collector of the pneumatic system. Finally, the aircraft's windshield, along with the ports and sockets located along the fuselage, have an ice prevention system by electric heating of each area. In addition, the front windows of the cockpit have a windshield wiper system that allows the surface to be kept free of raindrops during taxiing, takeoff, approach and landing operations. This system is called "Wipers" and is operated manually from the overhead panel. The operation of each protection for the aforementioned areas is detailed below.

The anti-ice system of the engines is operated manually from its control panel located in the overhead panel, next to the control panel of the anti-ice system of the wings.

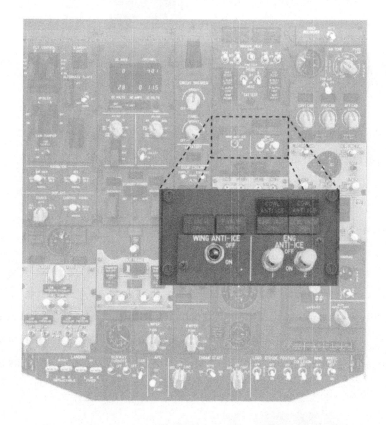

The control panel offers two system on and off switches. Above these, four visual indications are located. The two lower blue with the indication COWL VALVE OPEN, indicate that the valve for inletting hot air into the system is open. The two upper ones of amber color indicate COWL ANTI ICE informing that the pressure of hot air has exceeded the normal operating limit.

The operating principle of the system is based on the path of the flow of hot air from the engines, which passes through an inlet valve known as "Cowl Valve".

In this image, the closed valve is observed preventing the entry of the flow of hot air from the engine.

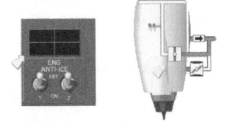

When the pilot activates the control panel switch, the valve opens and lets the hot air flow through to heat the area and the visual indication of the system lights up as a function.

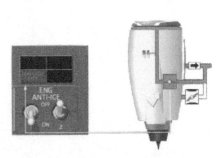

When the system detects an excess in airflow pressure, it activates the visual indication to warn pilots of this situation. This warning is presented in the system panel with the legend "Cowl Anti Ice", and in the main panel next to "Fire Warm" and "Master Caution" alarms with the legend "Anti Ice", indicating that the system presents an anomaly.

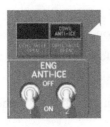
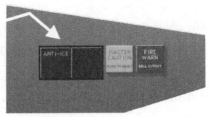

The anti-ice system of the wings shares the panel with the anti-ice system of the engines and presents the same operating principle. A single switch activates or deactivates the system, opening and closing a valve that allows the flow of hot air to enter, but in this case, from the pneumatic system.

The closed valve prevents the passage of the flow of hot air coming from the pneumatic system

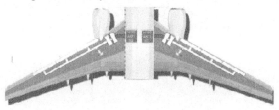

When the pilot manually activates the system by taking the switch to the ON position, the valve opens and supplies the entire heating circuit installed along the wing.

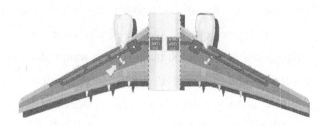

It should be mentioned that the system is operated for both wings at the same time, unlike the anti-ice system of the engines that allows the selection of the engine to operate.

Meanwhile, the anti-ice system of the windshield and windows shares the control panel with the anti-ice system of the aircraft sockets. This panel is located in the overhead panel, just above the previous panel.

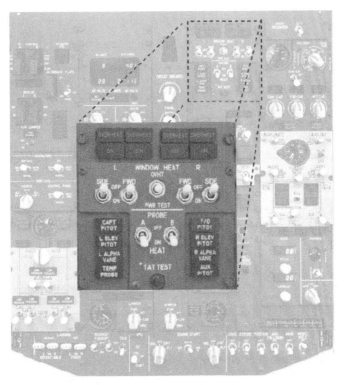

This system is based on heating the windshield and side windows through the electrical system. Each area can be heated independently, selecting the switch that the pilot wants, from the control panel. When the system is activated, the visual ON indication turns on just above the activated switch. When the system has a failure, the warning signal is activated with the indication OVERHEAT.

On the other hand, the anti-ice system of the sockets is divided into two, system A and system B, both operated from the same control panel. System A, supplies the left side of the aircraft and all its sockets. System B supplies the right side of the aircraft and all its sockets.

Finally, the system offers two windshield wiper devices that allow the front surface of the windshield to be kept free of raindrops for taxiing, takeoff, approaching and landing operations. It is operated manually and offers four positions. In the PARK position the system is disabled. In the INT, LOW and HIGH positions, the system is activated and divides its intensity into three variants.

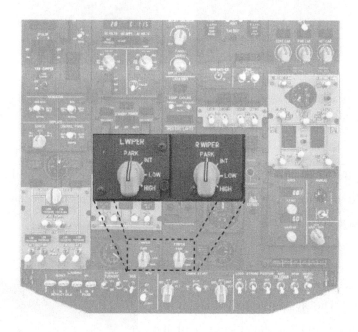

Autoflight system

The aircraft has a comprehensive automatic flight system that combines autopilot work, flight director and automatic power. The system has two flight control computers known as FCC (flight control computer) and are responsible for calculating the power, pitch and roll of the aircraft, according to the requirements established by the pilots from the MCP or "mode control panel".

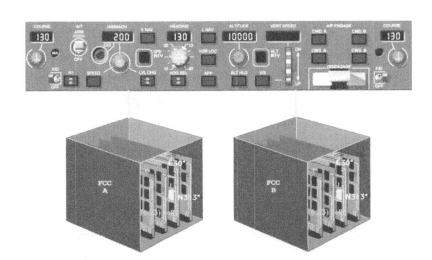

Each FCC is named A or B, giving this designation to each autopilot (AP). Additionally, it controls the bars of each flight director (flight director FD) and controls the adjustment of the acceleration levers according to the programmed power.

The system offers three levels of automation for the operation of the aircraft. At the minimum level of automation, FCCs only operate the flight director's bars during a flight operated manually by pilots.

At the intermediate level, the FCC operate autopilot and auto throttle, but being guided by the pilot's indications on the MCP.

The high level, where flight automation is total. FCCs control the entire operation, as established in the flight plan loaded into the system.

Each flight mode can be configured by pilots from the MCP, operating the corresponding section.

All flight modes are announced on the primary flight display, above the top section. This section is known as FMA (flight mode annunciation) and is divided into four sections.

The operation of the system is based on the selection of the different flight modes. Below is the operation of each part of the automatic flight system.

The flight director (FD) is activated manually from a switch located at the ends of the MCP. Without the FD activated, the primary flight display will not show the guide bars offered by the system. When the switch is activated, the FMA will show the activation information with the indication FD, but even the bars will not appear until the pilot selects a flight mode to fly. In this way, the DF system will understand what actions it must indicate to the pilot through the guide bars. The following example represents the three situations, ending with the selection of HDG SEL mode and the appearance of the FD bars.

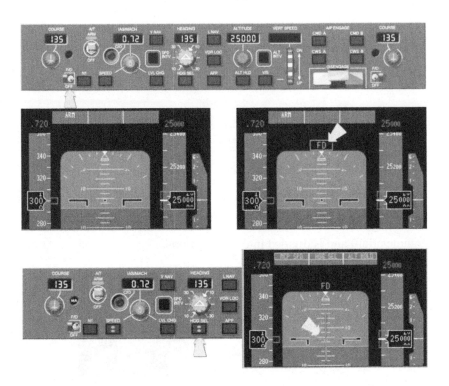

On the other hand, the autopilot or AP has two flight modes and are activated from the right section of the MCP. The main mode of the AP is command or CMD mode, being able to opt for CMD mode A or B (FCC A or FCC B). In this mode, the AP has total control over the pitch and roll of the aircraft. The alternative mode of the AP is the "control wheel steering" mode or CWS allows the pilot to intervene in the attitude of the aircraft by modifying the pitch and roll with the control controls, but still maintaining automatic flight. A function, usually used, to correct small changes in the direction of the aircraft, in order to avoid a storm front, etc.

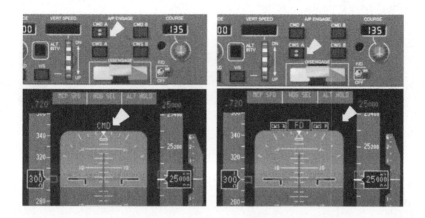

The disconnection of the AP can be carried out in three different sections, from the disconnect button located on the control controls, from the CMD button in the MCP or from the disconnection bar located under the activation buttons and identified with the name of "Disengage".

 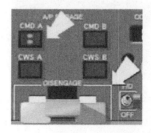

When the system detects that the AP has been disconnected, it emits an audible alarm and a red visual alert in the panel located above each inboard display or navigation display. These alerts inform pilots about the disconnection of the PA.

Finally, the automatic acceleration system or "Auto Throttle" or AT is activated from the left section of the MCP, actuating a switch from the OFF position to the ARM position.

Once the system has been activated, the FMA announces this new condition in ARM or armed mode, until the pilot selects SPD or speed mode to tell the AT system that it must operate a certain power for a certain speed.

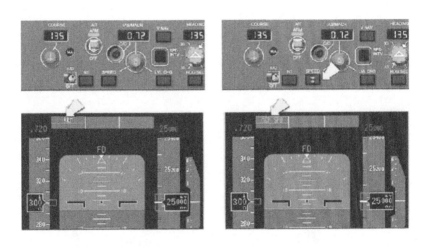

The disconnection of the AT system can be carried out on two different paths, from the activation switch on the MCP, or from a disconnection button located on the sides of the accelerator levers.

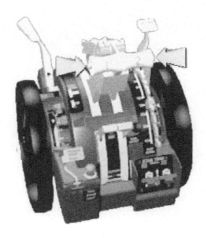

When the system detects that the AT has been disconnected, it emits a red visual alert in the panel located above each inboard display or navigation display.

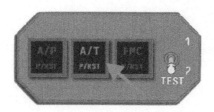

HUD Head up Display

The HUD system of the aircraft is based on an information panel where the pilot can find different types of flight data. It is formed by a transparent glass screen that allows the pilot to observe through it. As a result, it allows the pilot to continue looking forward, and at the same time, continue observing all flight information, without having to look down to see the primary flight screen. Hence its name, "head up."

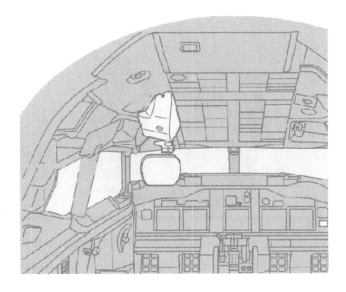

The system is composed of five components:

• HUD computer.

• Overhead unit OHU

• Combiner

• Control panel

• Annunciator panel

The system computer (HUD computer), receives all flight information from the aircraft sensors and its systems, converts this information into symbols and sends them to the control unit located in the overhead panel (OHU). From the panel, the information reaches the "Combiner" or glass screen where the entire symbology is projected, but without altering visibility through the glass.

The entire HUD system is controlled by a control panel located on the pedestal panel of the aircraft. From there, the pilot can configure the modes of use and manually enter the information he needs.

The system offers four operating modes with which the pilot can fly the aircraft under different conditions:

The primary mode or PRI: this mode is the most used and is suitable for all phases of the flight, from takeoff to landing, including low visibility takeoffs, non-precision approaches, precision and ILS CAT II.

Approach mode or AIII: used for ILS category II and III approach operations.

BMI mode: used for approaches operated with AP, DF and /T systems.

VMC mode: used for visual approaches.

In addition, the system offers the possibility of displaying TCAS system information and fault warnings within the display in any of its modes.

The OHU is the container of the display, allowing its extension and retraction. Add a rotating knob to adjust the brightness of the screen.

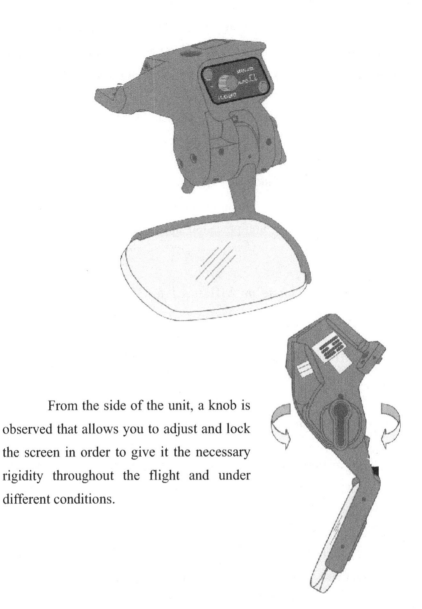

From the side of the unit, a knob is observed that allows you to adjust and lock the screen in order to give it the necessary rigidity throughout the flight and under different conditions.

The control panel offers various functions. A mode selection section (point 1), an informative screen (point 2), a light indication of system failure (point 3), a key line for brightness adjustment (point 4) and a numeric keypad for manual data entry (point5).

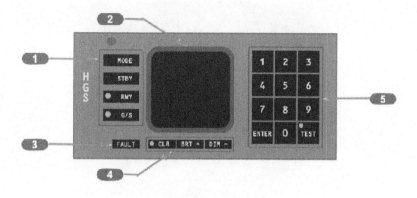

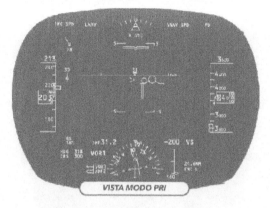

VISTA MODO PRI

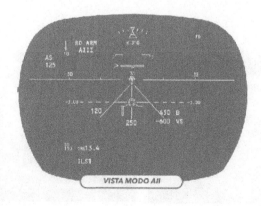

VISTA MODO AII

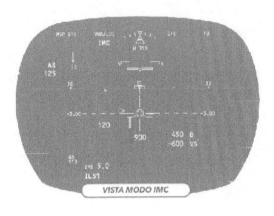

VISTA MODO IMC

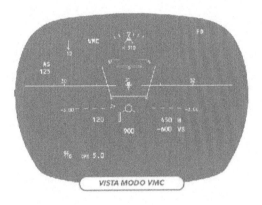

VISTA MODO VMC

Systems IV

B737-700/800/900

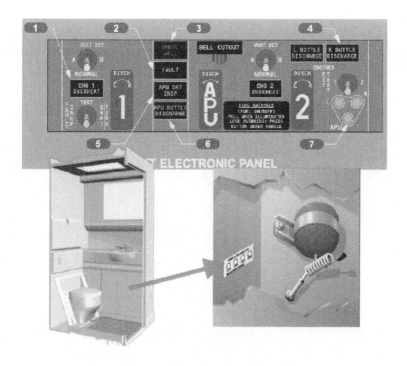

Fire Protection System

The aircraft is equipped with a fire detection and extension system in five areas: in the engines, in the APU, in the warehouses and in the bathrooms. In addition, the engines have an excess temperature detection system and the wheels of the main train with a fire detection system but do not have fire extinguishers.

Each engine is equipped with a duplicate detection system, a sensor A and a sensor B. When the sensors detect a temperature above the preset limits, they activate the overheat or overheating alarm. In case the temperature continues to rise to maximum values, the system will consider fire to exist and activate FIRE WARM alarms. The system is equipped with two fire extension bottles that can be unloaded from the fire protection panel.

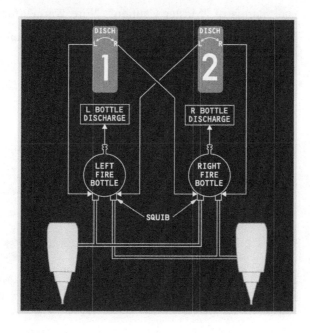

When the system detects an overheat, activate the "Master Caution" alarm, turn on the OVHT/DET light and turn on the ENG 1 (2) OVERHEAT indication on the fire protection panel.

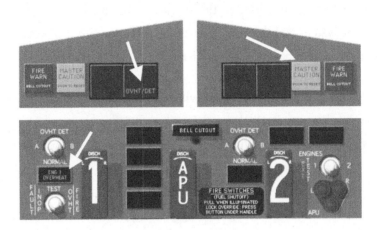

When the system detects fire, activate the audible alarm along with the visual alarms of "Master Caution", "Fire Warm", turn on the OVHT/DET light and turn on the ENG 1 overheat indication and turn on the red light of the affected engine number on the fire protection panel.

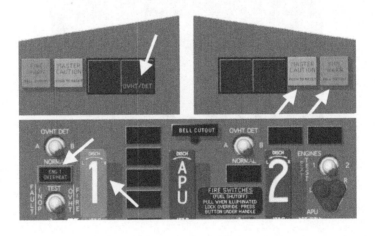

When detecting the engine affected by the fire, the pilot begins the firefighting process by lifting the switch of the engine number illuminated in red in order to activate the extinguishing system. When activating the system, the fire extinguishers are not yet discharged, the system prepares for download by performing the following tasks:

• Build the fire extinguishers.

• Close the fuel valves of the affected engine.

• Close the hydraulic valves of the affected engine.

• Close the pneumatic valves of the affected engine.

• Disable the reverse system of the affected engine.

• Cut off the power of the generator of the affected engine.

To discharge the fire extinguishers on the engine fire, the pilot must turn the switch to the left side, activating the left fire extinguisher; and to the right side, activating the right fire extinguisher until the fire is turned off. On the upper right margin of the panel, the visual indications of the discharged fire extinguishers will be activated.

For its part, the APU's fire protection system has a single fire detector and a single fire extinguisher. It works completely independent of the fire protection system of the engines although they share the same panel. When the system detects an excess temperature and assumes that there is fire in the APU, audible and visual alarms are activated. The Fire Warm alarm on the fault panel turns on and the APU switch on the lower fire protection panel lights up red.

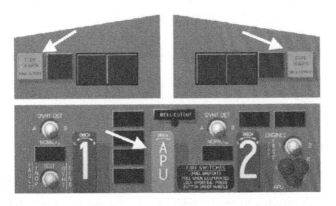

When the problem is detected, the pilot begins the firefighting process by lifting the red illuminated APU switch in order to activate the extinguishing system. When activating the system, the fire extinguisher is not yet discharged, the system prepares for download by performing the following tasks:

• Arm the fire extinguisher.
• Close the fuel valve.
• Close the pneumatic valve.
• Cut off the generator's power.
• Close the external air intake into the system.

Unlike the previous system, this system provides a single fire extinguisher to fight fire. For this reason, the pilot will be able to turn the switch on both sides and will have the same effect. To the left of the switch the APU fire extinguisher discharge indication lights up.

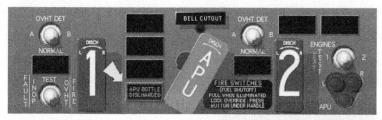

If necessary, a fire in the APU can be put out from the ground by maintenance personnel. Under the fuselage, on the left main train is an operating terminal of the APU fire protection system. From this panel, ground personnel will be able to perform the same actions as pilots from the cabin.

In addition, the fire protection system offers a detector on the main wheels of the landing gear. When the system detects this anomaly, it activates the FIRE WARM alarm, the audible alarm and a visual indication on the fire protection panel that describes the situation by illuminating a sign indicating WHEEL FIRE.

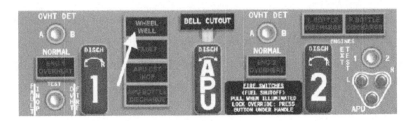

The system does not have a fire extinguisher in this area, so the only action that the pilot can consider is to extend the landing gear in order to allow the air flow to put out the fire or reduce the temperature of the wheels.

Meanwhile, the bathrooms have an automatic fire protection system. It is composed of a smoke detector and a fire detector due to excess temperatures. When the system detects fire inside the cabin, it automatically discharges the fire extinguisher located under the sink.

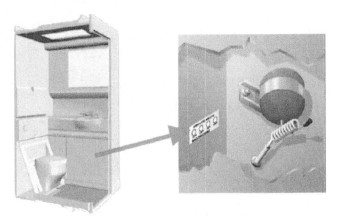

Finally, the fire protection system in warehouses. It is composed of two smoke detection sensors in each cellar (loop A and loop B). Smoke detectors in the holds are located on the upper panels of them along the fuselage of the aircraft.

Smoke detector installed in a pan (typical)

When the sensor detects smoke in holds, it activates the audible alarm in the cockpit illuminating the FIRE WARM panel. Once the pilot identifies the problem, he will be able to fight fire from the control panel located on the "pedestal panel".

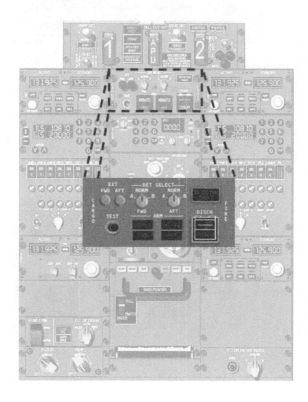

The panel has two rotating knobs, one for the front hold and one for the rear hold. In these knobs, the pilot can select the detection system he wants to use, A, B or in the NORM position letting the system select the detectors automatically. Under the knobs are the visual fire detection alerts, one for each winery. When the system detects fire, it activates the audible alarm and the light signal corresponding to the cellar that presents the problem turns on. In this case, there is fire in the back hold.

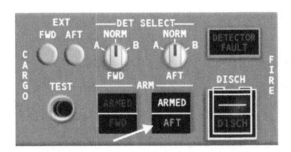

Once the fire is detected, the pilot should only remove the safety guard that covers the fire extinguisher button and press it to discharge the chemical on the fire.

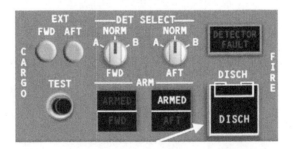

Flight Control System.

The flight control system is divided into two groups, the primary flight controls and the secondary flight controls. The primary controls are: the steering and depth rudder, along with the ailerons. Secondary controls are: spoilers and high lift devices (flaps and slats). Each of these flight controls is described below.

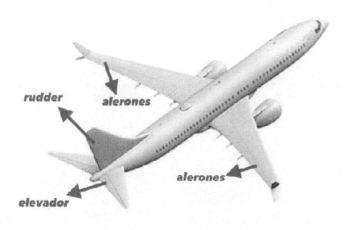

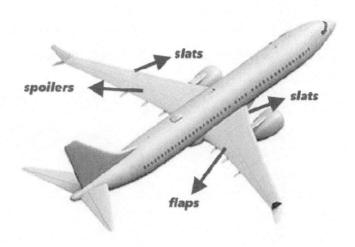

Secondary flight controls

Spoilers: these devices are located on the outside of the wing, that is, on it. They have 12 devices and are divided into two groups, flight spoilers (8 devices) and ground spoilers (4 devices), known as "Flight Spoilers and Ground Spoilers".

Flight spoilers can be used to help spoilers in their work of turning, or they can be used as speed brakes, reducing speed during a certain flight maneuver.

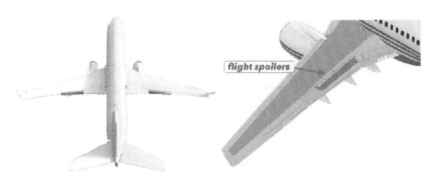

Meanwhile, ground spoilers work as brakes during the landing race or during the run of an aborted takeoff (RTO).

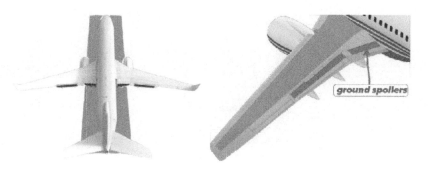

Spoilers are operated manually from the acceleration quadrant on the bottom panel or pedestal panel. When the pilot activates the spoilers, a light warning is turned on on the main panel, notifying of this situation.

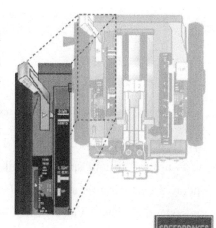

The entire spoiler system is operated by hydraulic system A and B, dividing these two systems between the 12 devices as follows:

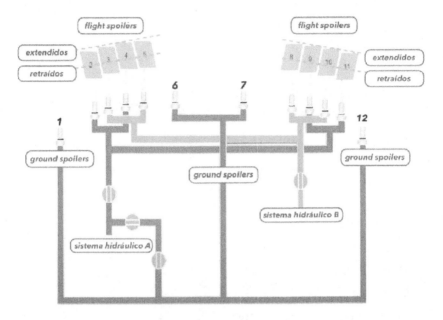

Flight spoilers 2, 4, 9 and 11 are operated by hydraulic system A, as are all ground spoilers, while flight spoilers 3, 5, 8 and 10 are operated by hydraulic system B. This operating scheme helps the pilot understand which devices he could lose in the event of a hydraulic failure. For example, considering a hydraulic failure of system A, the pilot could assume that he loses all the ground spoilers.

High lift devices: the objective of these devices is to increase the wing surface in order to obtain greater support at a lower speed. They are divided into two: flaps and slats. They are located on the leading edge and the leaking edge of the wings.

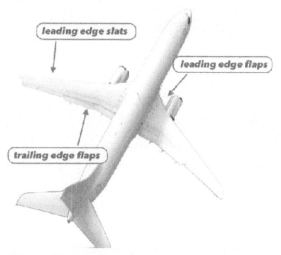

High lift devices are operated manually from the acceleration quadrant, with a lever on the right side of the panel. This system has several configuration positions, from 0 or completely retracted to 40 or completely extended.

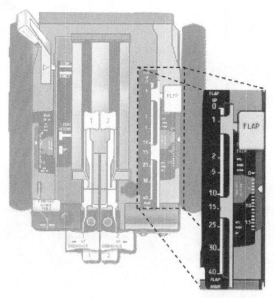

Starting with the devices located on the leading edge, each wing has a system of four slats and two flaps.

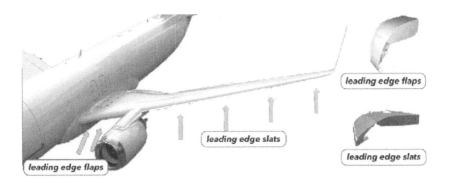

When the pilot activates these devices, a light warning is turned on in the main panel, notifying of this situation. On the overhead panel, the operating indicators are turned on with a color code, where the amber color indicates that the device is in transit and the green color indicates that the devices are extended.

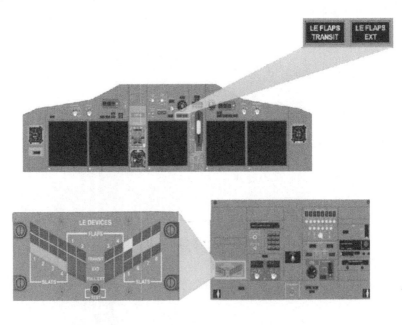

The entire high lift system is operated by hydraulic system B, being able to receive pressure from system A in case of any failure in the main system.

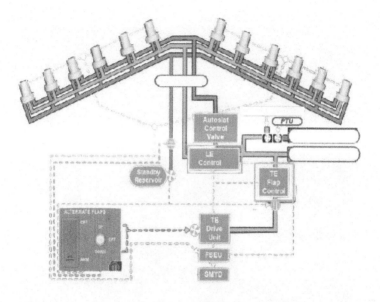

Passing to the back section of the wings, on the leaking edge are the flaps known as trailing edge flaps. They are divided into two, internal flaps and external flaps. Like previous devices, trailing edge flaps are operated by the hydraulic pressure of system B.

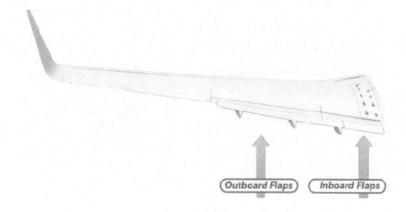

In case system B cannot comply with the operation of the flaps, the pilot can activate an alternative flap operation system from the control panel located on the upper left margin of the overheat panel.

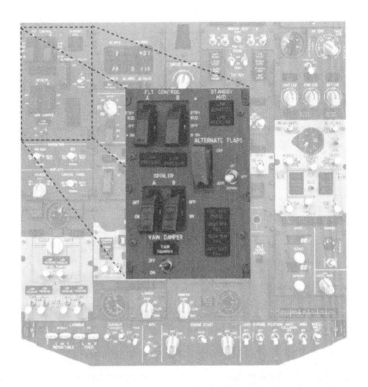

In addition, the system offers an analog indicator of the position of the flaps and is located in the central panel, above and to the left of the location of the landing gear lever.

Primary flight controls

Rudder: known as elevators, they are devices located in the aircraft's pawning assembly. Two moving surfaces that allow the plane's pitching movement.

The elevators are operated from the control column using a hydraulic pressure-operated cable system of system A and B. The control columns are connected with two units known as PCU (power control unit), and are responsible for regularizing the movements of the elevators. Each PCU receives hydraulic pressure from each system separately in order to avoid a total failure in case of loss of hydraulic pressure from a system.

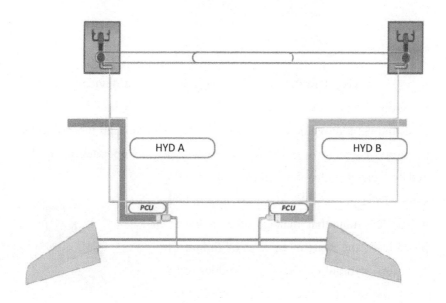

In case one of the PCU units fails, the rest will take care of the work and the pilot will be able to control the system normally.

In case both hydraulic systems fail at the same time, the cable system guarantees continuity of operation, requiring greater force on the commands to obtain the same results.

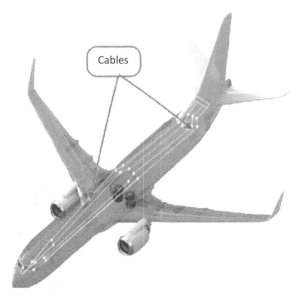

Cables

Steering Rudder: known as a rudder, it is a device located in the aircraft's empenaje assembly. A vertical and mobile surface that gives the wink movement to the aircraft. It works through the hydraulic pressure of system A and B. From the cockpit it is operated using the pedals located under the main panel on both sides of the pilots. Like elevators, the rudder has a PCU unit that manages the hydraulic pressure of the system. In case of failure of any of the hydraulic systems, the rudder has a standby system to be activated and replace the hydraulic system that has failed.

From the control panel located in the upper left margin of the overhead panel, the pilot can operate the rudder standby system, and even operate the hydraulic systems A and B that supply the rudder.

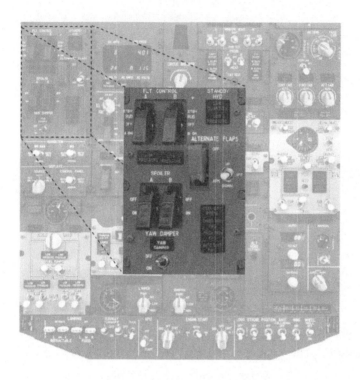

The steering rudder assembly includes a compensation system known as rudder trim. This system allows the pilot to configure a certain rudder deflection in order to compensate for an involuntary deviation. This system is operated from the control panel located on the pedestal panel. It has a rotating knob that allows the pilot to select the amount of degrees of deflection he wants.

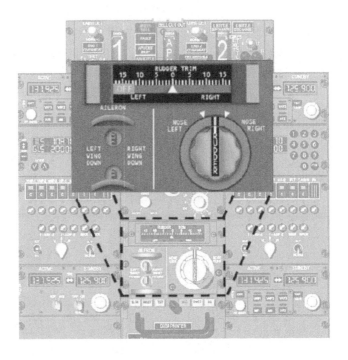

Ailerons: located on the leakage edge of each wing, they are responsible for allowing the aircraft to perform roll or warping maneuvers. The spoiler system works in conjunction with hydraulic systems A and B, which provide hydraulic pressure to command the movements that pilots require when moving the control levers from the cockpit. Hydraulic systems A and B operate the ailerons of each wing, dividing the work between the two systems by each plane. Like previous systems, the ailerons have a PCU unit that manages the hydraulic pressure that will supply the system.

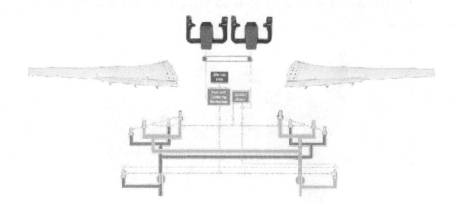

As in previous systems, ailerons offer a compensation system known as trim or airleron trim. This function allows the pilot to configure a certain wing inclination for one side or the other, trying to compensate for unwanted deflection such as straight flight with a stopped engine. The spoiler trim is operated from the same panel as the rudder trim.

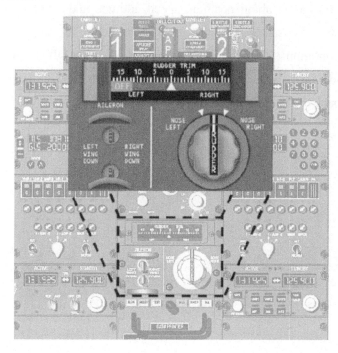

Its indication can be seen on the control column, behind the joysticks.

Inercial system

The aircraft system is based on an inertial system known as ADIRS (air data inertial reference system) that provides the aircraft with information about position, speed, altitude and attitude. All this information is used by different aircraft systems to inform pilots of the flight condition. The system consists of two main ADIRS, four flight data modules or ADM (air data module), and two control units located at the back of the overhead panel.

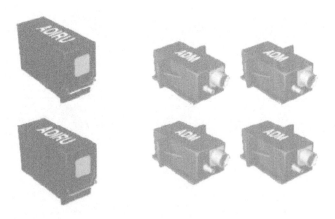

Each ADIRU offers two types of information, AD or air data and IR or inertial reference.

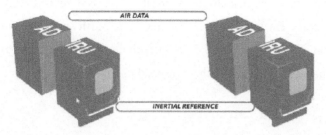

The inertial ones (IRs) replace the old gyroscopic instruments with which the aircraft was equipped. Each IR has electrical sensors and laser gyroscopes that measure the movements of the aircraft on its three axes, along with additional information such as: heading, vertical speed, ground speed (GS), course, high winds, and the most important information, the position of the aircraft at all times with the latitude and longitude values.

Each IR provides information to the instruments of the aircraft, the left IR supplies the instruments on the captain's side and the right IR to the instruments on the side of the first officer. Additionally, it provides information to the FMC (flight management computer) system for the calculation of navigation (to be developed on subsequent pages).

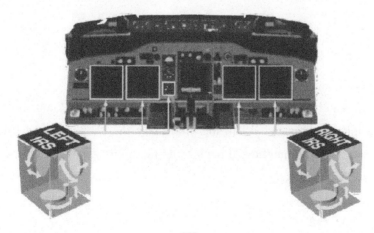

The inertial system needs to be aligned before being used. Prior to each flight, and with the plane completely stopped, the pilot begins the alignment sequence of the inertials. The system is based on the rotation of the earth to calculate the magnetic north and its position. The alignment process can take 5 to 10 minutes and starts from the IR control panel located above the overhead panel.

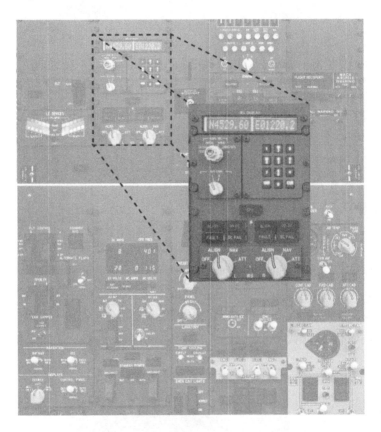

The bottom of the control panel has two rotating knobs to start the alignment process. When the pilot takes the knobs to the ALIGN position, the alignment cycle begins and the light signals are turned on with the word ALIGN.

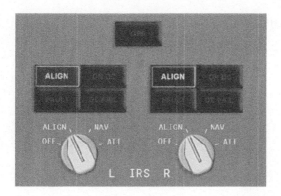

When the knob is selected in the NAV position, the inertial system switches into navigation mode, once the alignment cycle has finished. With the rotating knob in this position, the panel will not present light warnings, unless there is a system failure.

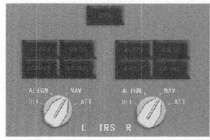 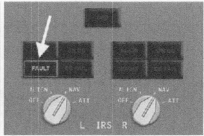

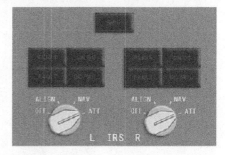

When the pilot takes the rotating knob to the ATT position, the inertial system will only offer information about the attitude and direction of the aircraft.

Finally, when the GPS signal is illuminated, it will indicate a failure in both GPS sensors.

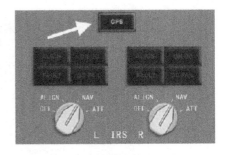

The inertial system includes a display next to a numeric keypad from where the pilot can enter the values manually into the system. Additionally, it has two rotating knobs, one to select the IR system you want to monitor (bottom knob) and another to select the type of information you want to obtain (top knob). The TK/GS position shows the course and speed with respect to the surface or GS. At the PPOS position, the current position of the aircraft is observed in geographical coordinates. The WIND position shows the direction and intensity of the wind. And in the HDG/STS position you can see the magnetic course and a status code for maintenance personnel.

Navigation System

The aircraft navigation system is based on a set of systems that work to position the aircraft and monitor its displacement, including: the flight management system or FMS (flight management system), the inertial system (ADIRS), the global positioning system (GPS), the radio aid system (AIDS), and additionally includes the transponder and meteorological radar system. The main system in charge of navigation is FMS and is composed of: FMC (flight management computer), AP (auto pilot), FD (flight director), A/T (auto throttle), IRS (inertial reference system) and GPS (global position system). While all these systems work independently, the FMS system regulates the joint work of each of them and pilots have a control panel to execute the necessary actions for navigation. These panels are located in the lower panel or pedestal panel and are known as CDU (control display unit).

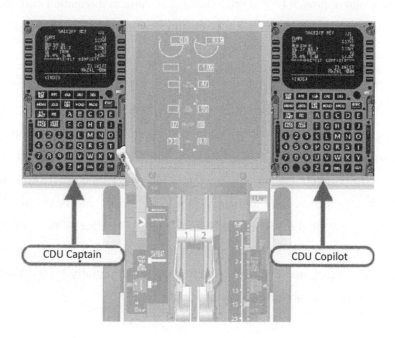

CDU Captain   CDU Copilot

The FMC system uses the flight plan information entered by the pilot, the information of the aircraft's systems, information from the FMC system's own database and the aircraft performance information to calculate the current position, pitch, roll and power required to fly an optimal flight profile. Once the FMC has all this information, it sends the orders to the AP, the FD and the A/T to perform all flight maneuvers according to the planned navigation.

The FMS system has different modes of operation. In its fully automatic mode, it offers lateral navigation control or LNAV and vertical navigation control or VNAV. When the pilot enters the navigation data to be carried out, the FMS considers all the sources mentioned above and plans the flight contemplating all the departure (SID) and approach (APP) procedures. For vertical navigation consider the optimal speeds, fuel consumption and recommended altitudes.

The FMC system offers a large number of variables that the pilot can manage from each CDU for each flight section, from shooting, takeoff, ascent, cruise, descent, approaching and landing. Although all the information is loaded only once into the system and it performs the flight completely automatically, the pilot can intervene in the management of the flight at any time, modifying data in the system, modifying parameters of each stage of the flight, taking manual, partial or total control, and even completely change the initially loaded flight plan, even if the aircraft is carrying it out.

The CDU module offers a series of pages for each flight stage, in which the pilot can load all the information he wants and needs to navigate. The first page of the system is INDEX. From there, the pilot gains access to the main pages for the initial loading of data.

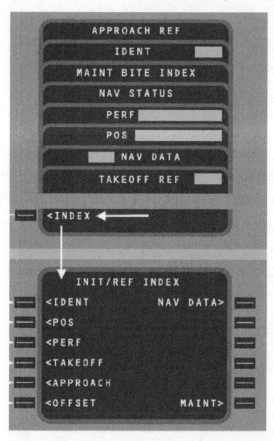

Within INDEX, the first option is the IDENT page or aircraft identification and the system database. From here, the pilot can verify the airplane model, the version of the program, the validity of the database and the initial position. On the lower left margin, the INDEX option appears again with an arrow to the left, indicating the way back to the previous page.

When returning to the main menu, the next page to verify is the POS option. On this page the pilot can verify the current position of the aircraft based on the information obtained from the IRs and the initialization of the FMC. They include geographic orientation data in latitude and longitude, airport information of your choice and an empty field to manually enter the position obtained from the IRs panel. As on the previous page and on all the remaining ones, the option to return to the previous page will appear on the lower left margin.

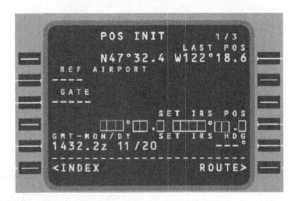

In this particular case, the page indicates an option to another page within the same configuration. Above the lower right margin appears the ROUTE option.

By entering this page the pilot finds the possibility of loading the airport of origin and destination with the ICAO designation of the same. When loading this information, the system will display the planned route in the database so that the pilot can accept, modify or reject it and load a new route manually.

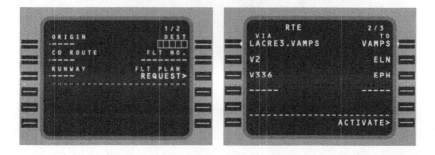

In case the pilot decides to accept the planned route in the database, it only remains to press the ACTIVATE button to activate the route and access the following pages within this already loaded route, in order to continue with the configuration of additional data for activated navigation. After activation, three more pages are enabled:

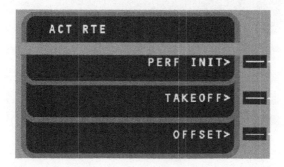

From the PERF INIT page, the initial flight performance data is loaded, such as: the GW, FUEL, ZFW, FL, etc., all data entered manually by the pilot.

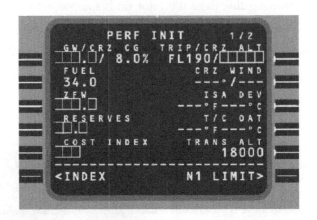

Once all the initial performance data has been loaded, the system will be able to perform all the calculations planned for navigation. When you return to the previous menu, the TAKEOFF REF page follows. From there, the pilot can load the information of flaps, speeds, trim, and access subsequent pages within TAKEOFF.

Even within the TAKEOFF page, the pilot can select the exit options or DEPARTURE options. From here it is possible to select the track to use along with the SID and the transition indicated by the procedure.

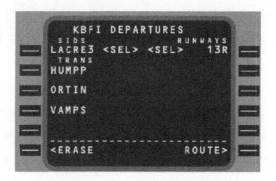

Once all the TAKEOFF load is finished, it is the turn to go to the ARRIVALS option where the pilot will be able to load all the arrival information at the airport, from the entrance load (STAR) to the approach letter (APP) as appropriate to the runway he plans to use.

Once the FMC system has received all the data entered by the pilot, it will already be able to plan the different flight profiles for navigation, looking for the optimal one for each phase of the flight.

Vertical Navigation (VNAV): on this flight mode, the system calculates a vertical operation profile, both in ascent and descent, and during the cruise stage.

VNAN mode controls the glide path and speed in order to comply with all the altitude restrictions that each point to fly over may have. Regulate the vertical speed in order to adapt each maneuver to the flight phase correctly and optimally for the performance of the aircraft. The following image shows the vertical navigation profile and the work of VNAV mode. After takeoff, VNAV mode is linked and begins to regulate the profile (PATH) and speed (SPD) in each takeoff and ascent pass until reaching the cruise phase.

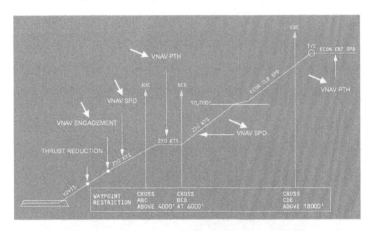

Although it is an automatic mode of vertical navigation, the pilot can partially intervene in the process and then continue automatically. In this example, the pilot intervenes in VNAV mode to level the ascent during a section and then continue the ascent to the final level.

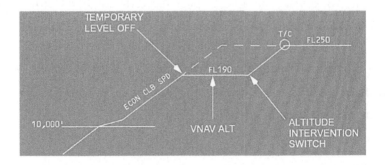

The operation of VNAV mode during the descent is identical to the previous operation. Vertical navigation is carried out automatically, according to the parameters established in the system and according to the optimal performance profile of the aircraft. The descent profile meets the restrictions of each point, and even provides an additional ascent profile in case of frustrated approach.

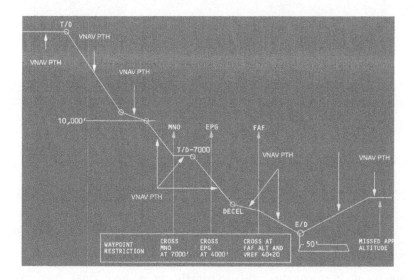

Lateral Navigation (LNAV): on this flight mode, the system calculates a horizontal operation profile for the entire route of the planned route. Horizontal navigation is carried out automatically creating a track to follow between each point involved in the route. The operating principle of horizontal navigation mode is the overflight of waypoints along the route. Each waypoint is created by geographical coordinates and is installed in the system database. In case the database does not have a certain waypoint, the pilot will be able to load it manually.

Waypoints are named five characters for points created on a certain position in space, and two, three or four characters for airport-based waypoints and radio aids.

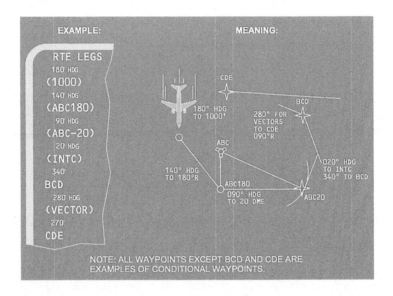

Radio Navigation (RNAV): finally, although the aircraft has redundant automated navigation systems, it also has the capacity and equipment to navigate radioelectrically in a traditional way. The frequencies of the radio aids are configured manually from the bottom panel or pedestal panel, where the pilot can select the frequencies of NAV 1, NAV 2 and ADF.

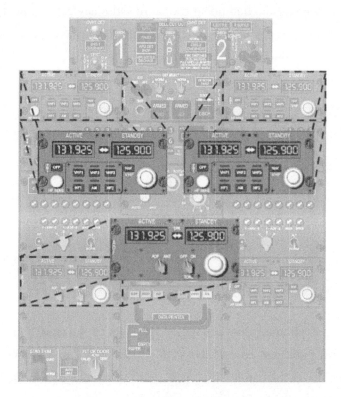

Nav aid information is displayed on the inboard displays of both pilots so that they can receive the same information.

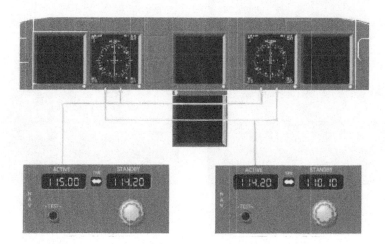

Based on the traditional format of radio navigation, the system offers different types of presentations on the ND (navigation display) screens. Each view mode can be selected by the pilot from the EFIS or ECP control panel.

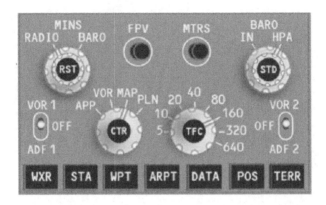

A traditional view of a digital HSI with all the radio information such as the selected course, the VOR 1 and VOR 2 station, the DME distance to each station, the ADF indication, the course deviation indicator or CDI and additional speed and wind information.

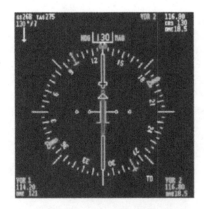 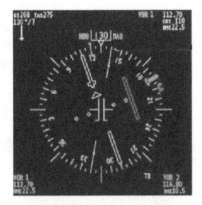

With the same information as the previous view mode, the system offers an expanded view of the information, diagramming an arc instead of a complete HSI.

Both in the view mode where a complete HSI is observed, and in expanded view mode, the ILS information of the locator and the trajectory of the glide path or GS is added, diagrammed with a column of points to the right of the view.

Additionally and as an aid to navigation, in expanded mode, the system offers the possibility of representing the information obtained from the weather radar, considering this view as a horizontal flight map.

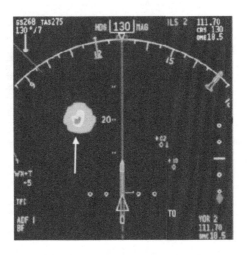

Oxygen System (Oxygen)

The aircraft is equipped with an oxygen system divided into two groups. On the one hand, the oxygen system for the cockpit and on the other hand, oxygen for the cockpit. Additionally, an oxygen tube system is incorporated as portable devices.

The oxygen system of the flight crew consists of an oxygen cylinder exclusively for the use of the cockpit and is capable of supplying four people inside the cockpit, the two pilots and two additional people (pilots in instruction, observers, instructors, inspectors, etc.). This system provides oxygen through special masks connected directly to the cylinder. These oxygen masks have a regulation system that allows mixing the air and oxygen that the pilot breathes, or activate oxygen 100%. Each mask includes a microphone to allow communication between the crew. Oxygen masks are located next to each seat of the pilots.

They are stored in a special compartment connected to the main oxygen tube of the cockpit.

The container box has an upper cover that partially covers the mask, allowing access to the test buttons and system activation switches. From these two switches, the pilot must pull upwards to remove the mask.

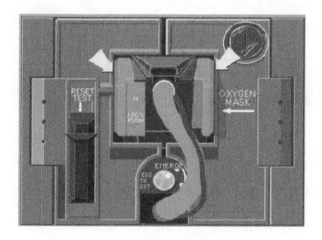

When removing the mask, an oxygen hose is connected to the main system. Once the pilot places the mask on his head, he will close the container doors and the system will start working.

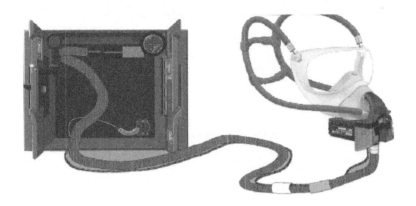

Although there are several models of oxygen masks, the standard and more complete model offers the following characteristics:

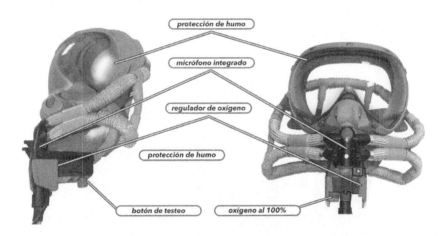

From the overhead panel, pilots can observe the oxygen pressure in the system using an analog indicator.

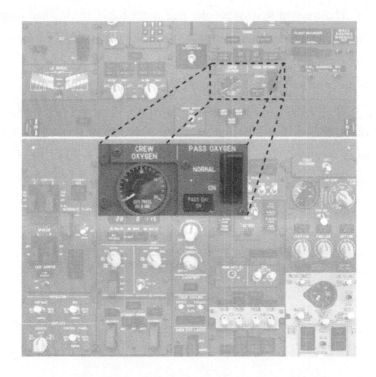

On the right side of the same panel, there is the oxygen system information for the passenger cabin. It has a visual indicator that announces: PASS OXY ON, when the system has deployed the oxygen masks in all rows of seats. On the right margin is a manual system activation switch, since this is an automatic system that is activated when the cabin pressure exceeds 14,000 feet. If necessary, the pilot will be able to manually activate the system, taking the switch to the ON position.

The oxygen system for the passenger cabin is obtained from a chemical generator located in three areas of the cabin: between the rows of seats forming a group of rows for each generator, at the positions of the cabin crew and in the bathrooms. The system is based on supplying oxygen to all people in the passenger cabin by using special masks that automatically fall from the top panel of each row of seats. This set of masks is activated when the person under them pulls down to place it on his face, covering his nose and mouth. This action activates the system and oxygen begins to travel through the ducts until it reaches the mask.

Made in United States
Orlando, FL
26 November 2024

54499140R00107